Y0-BFJ-622

PRELUDE TO FAME

PRELUDE TO FAME

An account of the early life
of Napoleon up to the Battle
of Montenotte

BERTRAM RATCLIFFE

Frederick Warne

First published 1981 by Frederick Warne (Publishers) Ltd.,
London, England

© Bertram Ratcliffe 1981

To my friend
Herbert Lom

ISBN 0 7232 2682 2

Typeset by Tradespools Limited, Frome
Printed in Great Britain
1531 · 1280

Contents

List of Illustrations

Acknowledgments

I am glad of the opportunity of recording my thanks to some for receiving me so courteously and hospitably in France, to others for their help when I sought additional information.

I am therefore most grateful to the following: Monsieur Charles-Alexandre Fighiéra, Conservateur of the Masséna Museum in Nice; André Lheritier of the Bibliothèque Nationale, Paris; Christian Bride, Commissaire de la Marine, Jean Le Gall, commanding Fort Les Six Fours, Jacques Lebon of the Musée Navale, Fort Balaguier (the last three all of Toulon); Miss Alison Gould, Head of the Information Department, The British Library; Madame Renée Derain of Dijon; Mrs Margaret Phillips, William Collins and Co; and Mr Ken Farnhill of York.

Chapter 1

The arrival

On the morning of 13 June 1793, a small coasting vessel flying the French flag passed unchallenged between the two forts guarding the entrance to the outer harbour at Toulon – La Grosse Tour to the east and l'Eguillette to the west – and glided smoothly towards the quay. At that moment a prayer of gratitude must surely have been breathed by the family of refugees on board, and by the Master too, for that matter; they had sailed from Corsica two days before across a sea infested by enemy ships. France had been at war with England since the previous February and British men of war were all around. Had the coaster been hailed and boarded, even had she been allowed to proceed on her way, one passenger would have been taken off and sent to England as a prisoner of war.

The passenger's name was Napoleone di Buonaparte, for so he was to sign himself during the next three years. In Corsica among his friends he had been known as Nabulio and the family name more often than not was written Bonne Parte. He was nearing his twenty-fourth birthday and proudly wore the uniform of a captain in the Artillery Regiment of La Fère. He was a small man, thin, with hollow cheeks, a sallow complexion and lank, untidy hair falling over his collar.

Since unforeseen events, even trivial happenings seem to guide the path of history, one may pause here to wonder what the future would have held for Europe had young Captain Buonaparte been invited to board a British ship on that June morning in 1793 and afterwards interned as a prisoner of war in England. What would not have happened is more clear. There would not have occurred the beflagged glory of the First French Empire, Waterloo would have remained an unknown Belgian village, Saint Helena a dot on the map of the southern Atlantic. There would have been no Napoleonic code of laws, no clear, high-thinking mind to bring order out of chaos, to lead men towards disciplined industry and fine achievement. The Napoleonic legend would have remained unborn, fewer Frenchmen would have died in battle, but they might well have found life less worth living.

Two other men, at the time young like himself, were destined to share the European stage with Buonaparte, one to blunt all his victories on land by victory at sea, the other to annul them by defeating him finally one afternoon on a muddy Belgian field. With the British fleet operating off Toulon during that summer under the command of Lord Hood in the *Victory*, was Captain Nelson in the *Agamemnon*, soon to be ordered to Naples on a mission of importance to England and of tragic significance to himself; for there he was to meet Emma Hamilton, a lady of unrivalled experience in amorous adventure, recently promoted from mistress to wife of the British Ambassador.

In Dublin Major Arthur Wellesley of the 33rd Foot was about to break painfully from Kitty Pakenham, burn his violin, give up cards and dedicate himself to the service of his country. He, like Captain Buonaparte, was twenty-four years of age. His decision led him to become the Duke of Wellington and the victor of Waterloo.

Meanwhile for those on board the ship moving slowly across Toulon harbour danger lay behind them and the green hills rising steeply above the town beckoned safety, such safety, that is, as might be hoped for in a country where nine men, calling themselves with supreme irony 'The Committee of Public Safety', had decided that the only way to ensure the happiness of those over whom they ruled was to terrify them into submission. Innocence now walked glancing over its shoulder, fear haunting every step; men never knew when a word or a look might betray a guilty thought; they no longer trusted in friendship; they listened, apprehensive, when footsteps mounted the stair.

Passengers with Captain Buonaparte were his mother, her half-brother, Archdeacon Fesch of the Ajaccio diocese, and six other children, three boys and three girls. The mother at this time was a widow, aged forty-two. She was of striking appearance, with large dark eyes, dark skin and clear-cut features. Her expression was stern rather than appealing. Before her marriage she had been Letitzia Ramolino. She came of solid stock, Italian in origin. Neither she nor the man she married belonged to the governing class, but neither were they peasants.

The Archdeacon accompanying the family was not of Corsican origin. His father, Letitzia's step-father, had been Swiss. Young Fesch – he was just thirty, young for an Archdeacon – had fled from Corsica with the Buonapartes, perhaps in fear of his life, more probably in the hope of helping his half-sister in her trouble. She did not truly need his help, though no doubt she welcomed it, for she had great courage, determination and sound common sense.

Of Napoleon's (we give him from now on the name by which history knows him) three brothers, Joseph was the eldest and should have taken the lead in family matters, but did not. Louis was fifteen, Jerome, the youngest nine. The three sisters, Maria-Anna, Maria-Paoletta and Maria-Annunziata, soon to exchange their Corsican names for Elisa, Pauline and Caroline, were respectively sixteen, thirteen and eleven. Pauline, already attractive, was to become truly beautiful. She had a loyal, generous nature, and a heart ready to blaze uncontrolled in moments of amorous enthusiasm, which in her case, were frequent. The other two girls were more intelligent but less attractive.

The ship's Master would have known all about their misfortune. They were in fact cousins of his, not that the relationship had any precise meaning, all Corsicans being cousins of one degree or another. (It is recorded that at least fifty turned up at Letitzia's wedding.) The Master certainly knew that tragedy had recently befallen the family and that they were now almost penniless. They had indeed escaped from their home in Ajaccio just in time, for within hours of their flight the house was ransacked by an angry mob, crying 'Death to the Buonapartes! Down with all traitors to Corsica and Paoli!' Paoli was the island's hero, the leader of all true Corsicans, who after twenty years of exile in England was once again among his people, fighting for their independence.

Letitzia and the younger children had found, with the assistance of Archdeacon Fesch, a hiding place along the coast from where, by an extraordinary chance, Napoleon rescued them and travelled north-ward with them to Calvi where friends still held control, and where

Joseph joined them. 'This country is not for us', said Napoleon, and in that moment cut himself off from his native island and became a Frenchman. Hastily the family sailed for Toulon.

The only Buonaparte not on board was Lucien, next in seniority and intelligence to Napoleon. Lucien had been in Toulon these last three months. It was he indeed who had done much to bring disrepute upon the family. By nature a facile speaker, by desire a red-hot revolutionary, he had developed his gift of oratory by making impassioned speeches at the local Jacobin Club. He had denounced Paoli as an enemy of liberty and demanded his arrest. Paoli had already lost favour with the Government and was promptly invited to Paris to explain his conduct. Everybody knew the meaning of such an invitation. Paoli, pleading ill-health, preferred the security of the Corsican mountains to an interview with the Committee of Public Safety followed by the inevitable ride to the guillotine. His state of health did not, however, prevent him reacting in a forcible manner when he received a copy of Lucien's speech. Already the Buonapartes had annoyed him by leaning towards the violent men in Paris. In particular Napoleon had irritated him by aspiring to be his right-hand man and possible successor. Napoleon's election as Lieutenant-Colonel of a battalion of Corsican volunteers at the age of twenty-two – while over-staying his leave from his regiment in France – was unpardonable. His country was at war, the country he had sworn to defend. Why had he not reported for duty? Instead he was playing at politics in Corsica. Corsica could easily dispense with the services of this ambitious, self-centred, thrusting young man. Paoli had had enough. True, Napoleon's father had been his friend twenty years ago, before his flight to England, true, he, Paoli, had more than admired his mother, the beautiful Letitzia. But the younger generation were impossible. They must go. The Buonapartes were accordingly proscribed as enemies and outlawed. Their fellow citizens gave proof of loyalty by sacking their home.

The Master of the ship could not know or even guess, as he steered them to safety, that within a few years this middle class family of refugees would blossom into one emperor of immortal fame, three kings, one queen, one princess, one grand-duchess and one scarlet-robed cardinal, for Uncle Fesch was not forgotten. Only Letitzia was to remain what she had always been, wise, courageous, steadfast, practical, never losing a sense of proportion.

Chapter 2

Charles the flippant

Before the vessel ties up alongside the quay at Toulon, one other member of the Buonaparte family must be mentioned, Charles, the father without whose pleasant efforts the family could not have existed. Charles, known earlier as Carlo-Maria, was eighteen when, in 1764, he married Letitzia Ramolino, she fourteen. Although it was Napoleon, the second son, who was to launch the family on its meteoric flight, his father had laid sound foundations for the launching. Charles died in Montpellier in France at the early age of thirty-nine, of what was probably cancer, though it was not diagnosed as such at the time. Yet had he lived it is doubtful whether his presence that day in Toulon harbour would have contributed much to the fortunes of his family. Having done his part in bringing into the world one of the greatest minds it has known, he would from now on have been forced to live in the shadow of the genius he had engendered. Being a vain man, feverishly active, though without industry, he must have found such a role increasingly irritating. In addition his courtly manners would have contrasted strongly with his brilliant son's occasional ill-tempered vulgarity, and to the latter's detriment.

Like most Corsicans of his day Charles was of Italian origin. He was of good appearance, slim, of moderate height, with a certain elegance. He wore expensive clothes to advantage and had a weakness for embroidered waistcoats. Everything had to be of the best. That he could not afford extravagance was of no consequence. It could be

5

embarrassing, but only until he had borrowed enough money from some soft-hearted friend to tide over the awkward moment. How comforting it was to feel that there were still people who realized that one had to live. True there were rumours of discontent, rumblings from below; the poor, it seemed, were very poor. But Charles Buonaparte's life ended four years before revolution could disturb it. He was comfortably out of the way when the storm broke in 1789.

In youth Charles had received an adequate education at Corte. After marriage he studied at the University of Pisa. Returning home to Corsica with a degree in law, he was appointed a minor judge at the Royal Court of Ajaccio, a position less important than it sounds, for at the time Ajaccio had a population of only four thousand, most of whom could speak no more than the local dialect. In any case the placid career of a lawyer in such modest surroundings had no appeal for Charles. Ambition led him towards a more colourful horizon. The point was how to reach it. In such cases luck is needed and the luck which befriended Charles Buonaparte was the acquisition of Corsica by France three years after his marriage to Letitzia Ramolino. During the previous four centuries Corsica had been a possession of Genoa, but declining power had led that state to part with the island in exchange for financial assistance. Genoa withdrew its troops which in any case were few in number and stationed only in coastal towns. For a short period it might have seemed to Corsicans, ignorant, courageous, resentful of foreign government, that they were now to enjoy a happy independence under their beloved leader, Paoli, whose life they knew was dedicated to their happiness and prosperity. But if declining Genoa had parted with an unwanted possession without regret, the new owner, France, was far from indifferent to her new acquisition. Corsica was to be part of France and Corsicans were to be Frenchmen whether they liked it or not. To convince them of the fact an active garrison of French troops soon arrived on the island. They were not welcome. They were, in fact, greeted with open hostility. Resistance arose everywhere and continued with some success during the following two years. But in the summer of 1769, when Joseph was about a year old and Napoleon soon to be born, Versailles decided upon sterner measures. The garrison was increased by the arrival of 50,000 men under a capable general, the Comte de Vaux, and in a single engagement, afterwards known as the battle of Ponté Corvo, Corsican resistance was crushed. Paoli and some three hundred of the faithful sailed for England, their departure not seriously impeded, possibly welcomed, by the French. Paoli remained in exile for the next twenty-one years assisted by a British Government which, having already stripped France of her colonial possessions was perhaps toying with the idea of adding Corsica to the list.

Charles Buonaparte, who had held a position on Paoli's staff, did not accompany his leader. Instead he took to the mountains with other enthusiasts, swearing to conquer or die in the cause of freedom. Upon reflection, however, he came round to a more reasonable line of thought. Seeing on all sides evidence of French military power and no sign of help from outside he decided that death or glory was not for him. Not that the admission implies cowardice; rather that common sense came to his rescue. Realizing where salvation lay he descended from the prickly discomfort of the maquis (which his brave wife had shared with him), executed a nimble pirouette and kissed the hand it had so clearly become unprofitable to bite. The French hand was wisely extended in friendship.

In later years Napoleon condemned his father's change of coat. 'He should have died for the cause in which he believed' – brave words. But Charles was right. Blind refusal to accept a rational truth which does not degrade the human spirit leads only to disaster. The passing years were to prove that the destiny of Corsica was bound to that of France, and to the profit of both.

The years, too, seem to have taught Napoleon that heroism is not all. When the opportunity came for him to act as he once thought his father should have acted, he failed the test. At Waterloo, when in the late evening the Guard advanced, heedless of death, towards the red lines on the crest, drums beating, colours flying, it was urged forward by the Emperor from the side of the road, but not led. And Prince Jerome, who fought that day with his brother, was heard to ask, 'Can it be possible that he will not seek death here?'

In Corsica pacification, not vengeance, was the invaders' policy; the island's population was to be won by kindness, or at least reasoned justice. Charles Buonaparte, educated, well-mannered, fluent in French and Italian, stood out among his rude, uncultured, if brave contemporaries as a desirable link between them and the authorities. He was among the first to be received by the Governor, the Comte de Marbeuf, with whom both he and his wife (Letitzia was not yet twenty) were soon on friendly if not intimate terms. Six years later when Louis Buonaparte was born and de Marbeuf became his godfather it was rumoured by envious or vicious tongues that there was a closer relationship, but the strict unbringing, the austere beauty and the sterling character of Madame Mère refute the charge. In addition de Marbeuf's amorous inclinations found ample satisfaction in the arms of his mistress, Madame de Varese, with whom he lived openly in true eighteenth century style, while his wife kept the home going in France. Madame de Varese, a lady of mature charms and considerable experience of similar situations, was well armed to protect her lover – as she would have put it – from the crafty designs of an uneducated peasant.

Meanwhile Charles drew profit from his association with the French Governor; for de Marbeuf quite naturally had influence at the Court of Versailles from which all good things flowed. 'Old School Tie' was an expression unknown at the time but it more than had its equivalent in *La Noblesse*, a privileged group of people who by accident of birth or dexterous climbing inhabited a realm where the necessities of life, spiced with pleasure, were to be had without the discomfort of daily toil. Once admitted to the sacred ranks of *La Noblesse* the aspiring candidate saw obstacles previously insurmountable dissolve before him, the upward road, previously steep, turn into a gentle slope along which he was wafted on a scented breeze. Such was to be the happy fate of Charles Buonaparte during the next sixteen years.

When armed resistance had virtually ceased, it was announced from Versailles that all Corsican subjects able to produce evidence of noble descent might in future claim equality with those of similar rank in France itself. Though in later years, when one of them became Emperor of France admirers set about providing them with a family tree, claiming descent for them from noble Tuscan ancestors, in the days when the Buonapartes lived in a narrow street in Ajaccio, nobody, including themselves, cared where they came from. In any case they could hardly be called aristocratic and Napoleon certainly gave little evidence of good breeding during his years of power, nor did he have much respect for those who relied upon ancient lineage for their station in society. He could afford to despise any such claim. He stood on firmer ground. Genius shone about him. And when First Consul he would rightly say, 'My ancestry dates from Montenotte' (the opening battle of his first Italian campaign).

Charles, his father, had fewer advantages with which to challenge the world. Nevertheless he made full use of such gifts as he did possess, and immediately after this tactful French offer he set to work to provide the necessary evidence of *Noblesse*. He had little difficulty. There rarely is when the requisite fee is available, and in the case of Corsicans the evidence required was unimportant. All one had to do was to produce proof that the family had been resident on the island through four generations. The majority of small landowners and many peasants and fishermen could have complied with this, though few incurred the trouble – or the expense – of doing so, regarding the offer as a bribe to win over their loyalty, which it probably was. Charles, however, was not of these. He set off to a good start by virtue of the fact that his degree in law in any case allowed him to claim *Noblesse de Robe*. He duly received his patent of nobility in September 1771, his son, Napoleon, being then three years old. Thus armed he began the pursuit of those material benefits within reach of *La Noblesse Pauvre*.

Charles Buonaparte excelled as a beggar, never openly requesting favours for himself yet in the happy position of profiting indirectly from those he sought for others. He cultivated the acquaintance of those in power, sought interviews with the minister of this or that department of state, or importuned his juniors with such persistence that from sheer exhaustion or for the sake of peace the victims scribbled a hasty signature across the petition in order to get rid of it.

Among other suggestions which Charles blithely put forward for his employment at the public expense was the cultivation of mulberries in Corsica. The venture was a dismal failure. He wasted much valuable time and money in pursuing an everlasting lawsuit against the Jesuit Fathers who he accused of sharp practice in the matter of a small parcel of land. He should have known better than to take on such a formidable opponent. Yet his charm and his distinguished appearance ultimately brought rewards and in due course he was chosen to represent the Corsican nobility at the Court of Versailles, in company with Monsignor Santini who represented the clergy, and a certain Casabianca who represented the Third Estate. Dressed with excellent taste, his sword at his side, he doubtless held his own among the genuine nobility of France who thronged the corridors and spacious galleries of the palace. He must have been a generous host, and an entry in his diary dated December 1778 gives some idea of how he considered a man of his rank and position should conduct himself. Corsica was not to be looked upon as a poor relation.

'I set off for the French Court with a hundred louis in gold. In Paris I received four thousand francs, a gift from the King, and a further thousand écus as a fee. I returned home without a penny.' The louis then being worth 100 francs and the écu 3 francs, the amount spent by Charles on that particular trip to Versailles was about 17,000 francs. It is difficult, if not impossible, to say what this would mean today, but a rough guess might be about £3,000. Meanwhile Letitzia, in Ajaccio, was scraping and saving every halfpenny. Small wonder that later in life when she found herelf in a palace, surrounded by servants and secretaries, she would say, '*Pourvu que ça dure*'.

Despite his failings, which were after all of a mild nature, causing him to flutter like a moth round the attractions of court and society, Charles Buonaparte should be remembered for having secured for his children the gift of education, for those at least who were able to benefit by his efforts before death intervened. The education he sought for them was not such as could be had in the half-civilized island of his birth, but the best enlightened, eighteenth-century France could offer. Filled with the desire to rise above the primitive surroundings of his youth he was equally determined that his children should not only rise with him but remain firmly on the higher level. Led by vanity as he surely was, Charles Buonaparte nevertheless held fast to the reins and made certain that vanity took him towards a rewarding goal.

In due course the two elder boys, Joseph and Napoleon, were admitted to the College of Autun, from where, after learning enough French to allow them to pursue normal studies, they were transferred to Brienne. Elisa at the age of seven entered St Cyr, the school founded by Madame de Maintenon for young ladies of good family. During the following eight years she remained there, mixing with the highest in the land, and no doubt she looked back on that period of her life with gratitude for the polish and assurance it gave her when she became Princess de Piombino. Lucien followed his brothers to Brienne. Nor was Madame Buonaparte's half-brother, Joseph Fesch, left out. A free education was obtained for him at the Seminary of Aix-en-Provence, from where he entered the priesthood and, propelled upward by his famous nephew, became in later years a Cardinal.

All this, including travelling expenses to and from Corsica, was paid for by His Majesty King Louis XVI in response to such heartrending appeals by beggar Charles as: 'I have seven children, Monseigneur, and am expecting an eighth, and I am almost without means'.

The fact that de Marbeuf's brother was the director of Autun no doubt accounted for the choice of that college as a starting point. It may be interesting to note in passing that Maurice Talleyrand-Perigord was at the time Bishop of Autun, waiting, as it were, in the wings for the little Napoleon to grow up and summon him to a career as brilliant as it was cynical.

Charles, having, as he would rightly have said, done his best for his elder children, died in 1785 without being able to see to the education of the four junior members of the family. He was spared the storm of revolution and the disappearance of all that meant so much to him; he was also spared the knowledge that his property had been confiscated and his family condemned by the Corsican authorities – with his old friend Paoli at their head – to 'perpetual infamy' and driven from their homeland. All this would have been too much for kind-hearted, shallow, flippant Charles. But what to Charles would have been tragedy, to his son, Napoleon, was opportunity.

Chapter 3

Corsica or France?

'This country is not for us,' Captain Buonaparte had said when he sailed from Corsica in June 1793. Stepping on to the quay at Toulon he could have said with even greater truth: 'Our future is here in France.' He was to return to Corsica only once and then not by choice: the ship bringing him back from Egypt six years later was forced to shelter from rough seas in a Corsican harbour. Corsica never had been for Napoleon. He needed a far wider horizon. He had, however, been a long time making up his mind to leave – so long that in the end the decision had been taken out of his hands. It would soon be eight years since King's Cadet di Buonaparte had been given his commission and ordered to join the Artillery Regiment of La Fère at Valence in the Rhone Valley.

Of his first seven and a half years in the Army Lieutenant di Buonaparte served only two and a half with his regiment. What his commanding officer, Colonal Dujard, thought of his frequent absence, his many requests for leave which he invariably over-stayed, is not known. He must have been an exceptionally patient man. But the time came when even he had had enough and Lieutenant Buonaparte, reported absent without leave, was dismissed from the Army. This we shall come to later.

At Valence his brother officers, drawn for the most part from wealthy, aristocratic families, were accustomed to being frequently absent on leave, which, in pre-revolutionary days, was granted liberally. Their requests for leave, however, bore no comparison with those of this young, penniless Corsican, of obscure background, who spoke French with a peculiar accent.

After serving an apprenticeship in gunnery for just over a year Second-Lieutenant di Buonaparte was due for four months leave. The four became sixteen, thus setting the standard he was to follow from then on. He appealed to the War Office in Paris, at the time under the direction of Marshal le Duc de Ségur, for an extra six months. His request was granted. His next move was to go himself to Paris, where, pleading ill-health, he obtained a further extention of six months. His health does not appear to have suffered from the long journey to Paris and back, nor to have prevented him from writing a *History of Corsica* after his return home. He sent the manuscript to Paoli, who received it coldly, saying that the young should not attempt to write history. When at a later date Joseph Buonaparte asked for the return of the manuscript Paoli replied that it could not be found. The younger members of the Buonaparte family were, it seems, already becoming unpopular with Corsica's hero.

Rejoining his regiment in June 1788, at Auxonne, where it was then stationed, Napoleon entered upon the most interesting and progressive part of his early career. Auxonne may be said to have been his university, the period of his youth devoted entirely to the acquisition of knowledge which, in his case, was to remain in his mind as in a store, ever fresh, ever crystal clear.

During his first sixteen months at Auxonne he worked as few, if any, young men of university age have ever worked. To his mother he wrote, 'I retire at ten (to save candles) and rise at four in the morning. I have but one meal a day, at three o'clock.' In later years he wrote of Auxonne, 'I lived like a bear in my small room, alone with my books who were my only friends.' Some idea of the wide range he covered may be gathered from the fact that while at Auxonne he filled thirty-six note books, thirty-three on history and philosophy, three on artillery.

If one meal a day sufficed his body, his mental appetite was insatiable. Nor was anything that nourished it lost. When confined to barracks for a minor fault, he found on a dusty shelf a copy of *Extracts from the Digest of Justinian*. In a few hours he had devoured the contents. Ten years later when, as First Consul, he was presiding over a discussion of the code of laws since known by his name and still in use over a large part of Europe, his companions were amazed to hear him quote passages from Justinian with ease and fluency.

By good fortune the School of Artillery at Auxonne when Napoleon was there was commanded by General Baron du Teil, an officer who was quick to recognize his intelligence and to give him every possible encouragement. This was remembered by the Emperor when, dictating his will thirty years later on the island of Saint Helena, he made the following bequest:

> To the son or grandson of Baron du Teil, Lieutenant General of Artillery, who before the Revolution commanded the School of Gunnery at Auxonne, we bequeath the sum of one hundred thousand francs in gratitude for the care this general bestowed on us when we served under his orders.

Not all admire dictators, but all must admire gratitude.

The sixteen months at Auxonne ended in October 1789 (the month in which Louis XVI and Marie Antoinette said goodbye to Versailles forever). There followed the usual request for leave, to be extended on one pretext or another until January 1791. In that month Napoleon returned to Auxonne taking with him his brother Louis, aged thirteen, whom he maintained out of his meagre pay. But their stay was short. Corsica called again; though this time with a definite reason. A National Guard had been formed on the island, thus providing an opportunity for impoverished but enterprising officers of the regular army to seek additional employment and promotion. The Colonel of his regiment accordingly received yet another demand for leave. This was becoming monotonous and the Colonel refused outright. Buonaparte proceeded to by-pass him by appealing to his friend and protector, General du Teil. The General persuaded the Colonel to alter his decision and he was given leave, but for three months only. Buonaparte must return to duty by the end of the year – December 1791.

But the favour was quickly forgotten. Before the three months came to an end Lieutenant Buonaparte had also become Second-in-Command of the Ajaccio Battalion of the Corsican National Guard. The appointment carried with it the rank of Lieutenant-Colonel. Aged only twenty-two, he was getting somewhere. But there was a price to pay for this lightning success, and it was high. Reported 'absent without leave'

14

by his Commanding Officer, he was, on 6 February 1792, dismissed from the army.

The floating balloon had burst. It was time for action. Joseph persuaded his brother that his only hope now lay in going to Paris and asking to be reinstated in the army. Napoleon agreed – indeed he had no alternative – and set off for the capital hoping for an interview at the War Office.

Once in Paris he renewed acquaintance with a school friend, de Bourrienne, later destined to serve him as secretary and afterwards as Governor of Hamburg. The two lived together at the Hotel de Metz in the rue du Mail, not far from the Tuileries where the King still resided, or more correctly, was imprisoned. More than two months passed before Napoleon's case was reviewed by the War Office.

While waiting for a decision he and de Bourrienne witnessed two notable events. On 20 June they saw the invasion of the Palace by the mob and the King obediently appearing on a balcony, a Red Cap of Liberty on his head. De Bourrienne recorded his companion's words when his Majesty came into sight, pushed forward by members of the mob, 'How could they allow that rabble to enter? A few cannon shots would sweep away a few hundred of them. The rest would soon take to their heels.' (In October three years later, the day of Vendemaire, Napoleon was to do just that and with the foretold result.)

On 10 August came a more serious, more tragic moment. On that day the two friends saw from a window opposite the massacre of the King's Swiss guards, Napoleon even running to save the life of one of them who lay wounded. He was horrified by the whole scene. Despite all, a sense of order ruled his life. This was not organized war but an opening of the floodgates to all that is most evil in human nature. He could not know that he was also witnessing the fall of the French monarchy, for the next day the King and his family were taken under guard to the Temple prison from where only death would free them.

Meanwhile Buonaparte's case had been reviewed by the War Office. He had not only been given back his commission but promoted to the rank of captain with effect from the previous 6 February, together with all pay and allowances. Strange that fate should ordain that one of the last acts of authority by King Louis XVI was to put his signature to the reinstatement in the army of Captain Buonaparte, who seven years later was to bring the monarchy back to life – after his own fashion.

That an army officer should receive back his commission after what amounted to desertion is hard to believe. There is, however, a possible explanation. France had been in a state of revolution for the past three years, and now revolution was gathering speed at an alarming rate. The *Ancien Régime* had gone up in flames and there was nothing to take its place but a flood of ideas without the leadership necessary to give them effect. No man knew what the next day might bring. Emigration fed by fear was growing to a torrent, more especially among army officers. Out of a total of nine thousand in 1789, by 1793 six thousand, Lafayette among them, had either resigned their commissions or fled the country. At the time when Napoleon sought reinstatement things had not reached this stage, but they were bad enough. He was forgiven, even welcomed. At least he had remained faithful to the oath of allegiance to the Constitution of 1791: to France, to the Law, to the King – in that order. Again he had brought with him from Corsica written evidence of his devotion to republican ideals and his acceptance of the union of his native island with France, when so many of his compatriots, following the lead of Paoli, stood for independence. And so by the first week in September, during which the rakings of the Paris slums, unchecked if not encouraged by the Minister of the Interior, Danton, broke into the prisons and hacked to death about half of the two thousand, six hundred prisoners detained in them, Captain Buonaparte, secure in the knowledge that his name would once more appear in the list of regular officers and that six months' back pay stood to his credit, was free to rejoin his regiment. It was essential that he should do so, for the Duke of Brunswick, with an army of 70,000 men drawn from Austria and Prussia, had invaded north-eastern France. That they were stopped at Valmy on 20 September made little difference. Danger was at hand. Every French officer and soldier must have felt the call to duty.

But not Captain Buonaparte, who again made his way back to Corsica. An excuse was at hand. An excuse of one sort or another usually is, and in this case it was provided by his sister, Elisa, who was still a student at St Cyr. This school for young ladies, established by royalty and paid for out of the royal purse, had come under suspicion and was about to be closed. How was Elisa, aged fifteen, to travel across a country where disorder, if not anarchy, reigned at every turn? The answer was clear – at least to her brother. He must accompany her. It would suit both admirably. The local mayor was persuaded to this view and signed a certificate ensuring them protection by official bodies, and, what was even more attractive, all travel expenses until they reached home. Napoleon and Elisa duly arrived in Corsica on 15 October 1792.

Valence was far away, as was his regiment and any thought of serving his country at war; for his country was not France even though it had given him a free education and was now providing him with a captain's pay; his country was Corsica, at least he was determined it should be. In Ajaccio he resumed his employment as second-in-command of the 2nd Battalion of the National Guard, a motley crowd of half-trained soldiers, which incidentally was to bring him into conflict with units of the regular army; indeed with nearly all Corsica. How it ended we know. A troubled eight months went by, months of undisciplined conduct, of straying up fruitless paths leading only to undignified flight.

Yet all was not profitless. For during those last months in his homeland, friendship, or a common interest, drew together Napoleon and a Corsican lawyer twelve years his senior named Saliceti. Of advanced political views, Saliceti had been selected to represent the Third Estate of Corsica when the States General met at Versailles in 1789. Later he became a member of the Convention and it was he who proposed the return of Paoli from exile in England. Paoli duly returned and was received in triumph. Afterwards, however, things had not gone according to plan. Paoli proved to be a disobedient child of the Revolution and three and a half years later Saliceti headed a mission sent from Paris with governmental powers to bring him to heel. In this difficult work Saliceti was assisted by Lieutenant-Colonel Buonaparte commanding the half-trained enthusiastic National Guard. The mission failed and Saliceti, like Napoleon, had to make a hurried departure from Corsica. But a few weeks later fate drew the two men together again, this time with consequences undreamt of by either, which would bring death, destruction and untold sorrow to millions, while overhead floated the flag of glory.

Chapter 4

Toulon in revolt

Revolutionary France, filled with the desire to free the world from the tyranny of kings and substitute her own, had begun this uphill work by declaring war on her nearest neighbours. However, before exchanging blows beyond her frontiers it was necessary to convert those within them whose interpretation of the words 'liberty', 'equality' and 'fraternity' was clearly at fault. Ignorance at home and obstinacy in the family must be overcome before the great work could triumph in less favoured parts of the world. But after nearly four years of revolution, after the monarchy had been overthrown, a republic proclaimed, privileges of the clergy and nobility abolished, and a host of reforms introduced, everywhere in France there seemed to be ungrateful men who refused to accept the gifts so generously offered. In Brittany there was open resistance; in the Vendée, south of the Loire, armed rebellion. The cities of Caen, Nantes, Bordeaux, Lyons, Avignon and Marseille rose in turn against the central government in Paris, which by the summer of 1793 was reduced to a most unholy trinity; for the National Convention, freely elected in the autumn of 1792, found itself too overloaded by argument and discussion of detail to deal with events (the execution of the King among them) which increasingly threatened its existence. Control was therefore handed over to nine men – the Committee of Public Safety – which in turn bowed to the dictatorship of three: Robespierre, Saint Just and Couthon.

Its leader was the virtuous Robespierre, so virtuous that to his tightly corseted mind anyone who disagreed with him disagreed with virtue and must therefore be destroyed before the infection could spread to others. Second in importance, though unfortunately not in influence, was the 24-year-old Saint Just, whispering youthful fanaticism into his leader's ear, counselling immediate bloodthirsty action where his leader might pause to consider legality. Third, but only by a hair's breadth, was Couthon, crippled in mind as in body, and of religious convictions which made him more rather than less dangerous to the enemies of virtue. Applauding the leader's every word before it was spoken, he frowned in advance upon the victims of his wrath; for was not Robespierre the chosen of God, the prophet come to change human nature and beautify the world?

Led by such men the Government overcame resistance. Paris, from its central position, was able to select at will where next to strike. The provincial cities were in turn crushed and vengeance wreaked upon all those foolish or ungrateful enough to refuse what was good for them. In Lyons leading citizens and others of suspicious conduct, or any heard to utter rebellious words, were lined up against a wall and shot. In Nantes representative Carrier, sent out from the Convention *en mission* with instructions to exercise his powers with *une sévérité inéxorable*, loaded barges with priests and nuns – always a tempting target for reformers – and with other enemies of the people, had them pushed out on to the Loire and sunk, a method of execution less rapid but more economical than shooting. That Carrier was to have his own head cut off a year later could be of no consolation to his victims as their piteous cries echoed over the water.

Towards the end of August 1793 resistance in Marseille was put down by General Carteaux, ex-house-painter turned soldier and recently promoted a general, though for what reason nobody could guess. He was an amiable, vain, stupid, comic-opera character, and his name is recorded only because Captain Buonaparte was very soon to come under his orders.

Carteaux was accompanied in Marseille by Commissioners, that is by members of the Convention *en mission*, formidable men empowered to place generals commanding armies under arrest, should they judge them incompetent, and have them sent to Paris for trial and probable execution, '*pour encourager les autres*'. Equally they could have all rebels, or any who appeared to them to be rebels, put to death.

They were men of terror. One must walk carefully in their presence, and as often out of it, for where terror stalks informers gather. The Commissioners accompanying Carteaux were Barras and Fréron, names not unknown to history.

Paul Barras was a *vicomte* of the *Ancien Régime* who had prudently dropped his title. His was not an enviable character. He was a seeker after pleasure and good living by all and any means. When young he had served in the Army, in the Régiment de Pondicherry in India, and, returning home after five years, had resigned his commission and drifted here and there while his or his parents' money lasted, after which, to use his own words, he accumulated a few debts. He came within an inch of marrying Madame de la Motte Valois, not the lady who brought dire trouble to Cardinal de Rohan and Marie Antoinette in the matter of a diamond necklace, but her sister who had managed to convey to him the impression that she was an heiress. Soon after this lucky escape came the fall of the Bastille, which he witnessed, and friendship with leaders of the revolution such as Mirabeau. Sensing which way the wind was blowing, Barras joined the Jacobin Club as one of its first members. Two and a half years after this mission to the south, he was to become the leading spirit of the Directoire, and as such to appoint General Buonaparte to the command of the army in Italy.

Fréron, companion to Barras (the Committee of Public Safety seems always to have sent out representatives in pairs, a prudent measure, for then they could report on each other) was also about forty. Although not of the nobility he was well connected and could boast that Stanislas, one-time King of Poland, was his godfather. He was lecherous, treacherous and a blood-thirsty revolutionary. In due course he came to know Pauline Buonaparte, the light-hearted, ignorant, eagerly amorous sister of Napoleon, who fell madly in love with him. (Pauline always fell madly in love.) When the undesirable Fréron asked for her hand in marriage, he was wisely warned off by Letitzia, and Pauline, though broken-hearted, escaped an unpleasant experience. Her brother subsequently chose for her General Leclerc, destined to die in the West Indies, and afterwards an Italian nobleman, Prince Borgese, who, though not endowed with brains, had good manners.

On 25 August Barras was able to report to Paris: 'All quiet in Marseille and the infamous rebels suitably punished.' Paris heads nodded approval, then stopped; for bad news, the worst possible news, followed quickly. Toulon, a bare two days later, had gone over to the royalists and had proclaimed as the legitimate King of France, Louis XVII, the little boy who, after the death of his father, was still a prisoner in the Temple.

An Anglo-Spanish fleet sailed into the great harbour of Toulon unchallenged by the French warships at anchor there. A mixed force of five thousand marines and infantry was landed and was soon reinforced by another twelve thousand. Toulon, on which France's Mediterranean fleet depended, had fallen into the hands of the enemy. It might be true that the town's inhabitants would have preferred to be liberated by Frenchmen instead of seeing the British flag hoisted over the Town Hall, but that was small consolation for the Committee of Public Safety. The threat could not have been more serious. Lyons and other cities were still holding out; this last rising would encourage them, even lead other centres to follow their example. At all costs Toulon must be retaken and without delay. Delay there was, due for the most part to the inefficient leadership of such men as Carteaux, for a lesser part to lack of guns.

But all, as far as revolutionary France was concerned, was soon to be put right. A young artillery officer recently arrived from Corsica provided the answer, as soon as he could make his voice heard.

Chapter 5

Saliceti waves his wand

On arrival in France Signora Buonaparte, penniless and with five children to care for, needed all her courage. Refugees from rebellious Corsica were certainly welcomed, but more than kind words and the playing of the National Anthem is needed by the hungry and the homeless. More indeed was given. After some delay financial assistance was provided by the Paris authorities and Napoleon, to his credit, spared what he could from his pay.

At the outset, however, it was no doubt Lucien who provided the essentials for his mother and younger brothers and sisters. Lucien, having been in Toulon for three months, was well in with the revolutionary party; he would have had friends and known his way about; he would have heard of, or been recommended to, Madame Cordeil who let rooms in La Valette, then a village on the eastern outskirts of Toulon, now part of the city itself; for it was here that the family found refuge, and where they stayed for the first few weeks, that is until the political atmosphere around them became too hot and the royalists took over power in the region. They then moved to Marseille by a roundabout route, pausing on the way at Brignoles, past which motorists today race in a furious stream towards the Riviera.

Meanwhile Joseph had made his way to Paris where fate was waiting to favour him. He arrived when all was turmoil; for while he was travelling from the south a young woman called Charlotte Corday was on her way eastward from Normandy to the same destination. Their aims were very different, his to seek help from friends or fellow Corsicans in power, hers to end once and for all the fevered writing of Friend-of-The-People Marat, who, like some monstrous toad croaking envy and hatred, filled every column of his paper with incitement to violence and death. As yet the butcher's knife which was to bring him death lay on a shelf in Monsieur Bardin's shop in an arcade of the Palais Royal. But on the morning of 13 July Charlotte was to enter and buy it, hide it under her cloak, drive in a cab to Marat's home across the river in the rue des Cordeliers and thrust it into his heart.

Joseph, arriving in Paris that day, cannot have failed to learn of the tragedy; he may even have seen something of Marat's state funeral the following night, when, lit by torches, the procession passed along the Paris streets followed by members of the Government and a great crowd of the poor and hungry whose wailing and cries for vengeance rose at intervals above the beat of muffled drums. Vengeance there was to be, the Committee of Public Safety would see to that; but the poor would still remain poor and the hungry without bread. Revolutions may add to human misery, they do not cure it.

Did Joseph see Charlotte seated in a tumbril, her hands tied behind her, looking neither to right nor left, on her way along the rue Saint Honoré to death in what is now the Place de la Concorde, by some admired, by some despised, surely by all pitied?

Whether Joseph Buonaparte was caught in the floodlight which shone momentarily upon Jean-Paul Marat and Charlotte Corday we do not know, nor is it important to the destiny of Napoleon Buonaparte. What was of importance was Joseph's chance meeting in Paris at this time with that fellow Corsican and friend of the family, Christophe Saliceti.

Returning from his fruitless journey to Corsica during the earlier part of the summer, Saliceti had taken his place again on the benches of the Convention, voting no doubt, as other members wisely voted, in favour of any and every idea put forward by Robespierre and his two satellites. (He had voted for the death of the King in the previous January.) Yet Saliceti had his good points. He was helpful to friends in trouble, and to his credit he found time not only to endorse a request for financial assistance to Corsican refugees in need, which the Convention speedily voted to the tune of half a million francs, but to come to the immediate help of individual members of the Buonaparte

23

family. Accordingly, by September Joseph was installed as a Comptroller of Army Supplies, Class 1, no doubt a lucrative position; Uncle Fesch, discarding his cassock for the occasion, was a storekeeper at Le Beausset, west of Toulon; Lucien was a storekeeper at Saint-Maximin, between Aix-en-Provence and Brignoles, where in addition he became President of the local Jacobin Club, practised revolutionary eloquence, and in a moment of enthusiasm adopted the name of Brutus. The presence of Lucien-Brutus near Brignoles may well have accounted for the halt his mother and the younger children made there on their journey from La Valette to Marseille.

But Saliceti had not yet finished waving his wand over the Buonaparte family, and his final wave was the most important of all, for it concerned Napoleon whose foot he was to set upon the first rung of the ladder that led ever upward until it collapsed under the weight of fame and power.

By chance, shortly after his meeting with Joseph Buonaparte in Paris Saliceti was appointed Commissioner to the army of General Carteaux in the south. After subduing resistance in Marseille and handing over that city for 'suitable punishment' to Commissioners Barras and Fréron, Carteaux's army had turned and marched on rebellious Toulon. By the end of the first week in September Carteaux had reached and captured the small town of Ollioules, some five miles west of Toulon. That, however, was the limit of his advance, and was to remain so for the next three months. At Le Beausset, where, it will be remembered, the Reverend Fesch was in charge of military stores, Saliceti and his twin Commissioner, Gaspari, had established their office. It was within easy reach of Ollioules which allowed them to keep an eye on Carteaux, but not inconveniently near the enemy.

After reporting for duty at Headquarters in Nice, Captain Buonaparte was posted to No 12 Company at the 4th Artillery Regiment. Luck was with him, for the general commanding the coastal batteries happened to be du Teil, brother of the Jean du Teil who had formed such a high opinion of him four years earlier at Auxonne. By General du Teil's order he was employed at Avignon where he was to organize the supply of ammunition for the Army of Italy due to operate eastward of Nice. It was then, in the vicinity of Avignon, that he wrote his dissertation on revolution entitled *Le Souper de Beaucaire* which Commissioners Saliceti and Gaspari promptly ordered to be printed and published at public expense, but which Napoleon, five years later, on becoming First Consul, ordered to be destroyed whenever and wherever found, its contents being too fiery for ordered society. Meanwhile the views it expressed brought Captain Buonaparte into favour with the Committee of Public Safety far away in Paris, which was what mattered to him at the time. The Committee may also have influenced a decision made shortly afterwards by Commissioner Saliceti, certainly the most important decision of his life.

Seated in his office at Le Beausset Saliceti heard announced a visit from his friend of Corsican days, now Captain Buonaparte, who had stopped off on his way from Avignon to Nice. The day was 7 September and the Commissioner, powerful or not, was worried. It was true that Ollioules had been taken by the Revolutionary forces and the line of battle pushed a few miles beyond, but in the course of action the officer commanding the artillery, Major Dommartin, had been seriously wounded. There were not many guns, some thirty in all, and they were of small calibre, useless in seige warfare. It was essential to replace Dommartin by a competent officer; for neither Carteaux nor anybody around him had the remotest idea of the employment of artillery. Sudden the very man appeared. He was young, barely twenty-four, but he was a first-class soldier, and he knew all there was to know about guns. Saliceti did not hesitate to offer the command of the artillery of Carteaux's army to Napoleon, and immediately reported his decision to Paris, confident that it would be endorsed by headquarters; for after all he was the man on the spot, the Government's personal representative. Napoleon, needless to say accepted. At last he had got command of men in action, the work for which he knew he was fitted before all else, in which he was determined to succeed. How fittingly brother Lucien-Brutus, witnessing the interview at Le Beausset, could have cried with fervid enthusiasm, 'There is a tide in the affairs of men, which, taken at the flood leads on to fortune.'

Chapter 6

The first command

The thin, lank-haired young officer hurried from the Commissioner's office in Le Beausset and set off toward Army Headquarters. The road led, as it does today, across land more or less level for some two miles, then upward between wooded slopes, and down again into Ollioules. He was never again to serve with the 4th Artillery Regiment. If his destination when setting off from Avignon with a convoy of ammunition had been Nice, he did not reach it. The convoy had to get there in charge of the next senior officer who duly reported to Colonel Dujard. The Colonel learnt, through the usual channels, of Captain Buonaparte's posting to the command of the artillery of the army attacking Toulon. Good luck to him. He was off his hands.

Arriving at Ollioules Napoleon reported to affable, vain, stupid, *sans-culotte* General Carteaux – *sans-culotte* because he owed his promotion solely to his revolutionary ideas and conduct – and presented his credentials. Signed by Commissioner Saliceti, they would have ensured him a cordial reception, though in this case, judging from his words, it is doubtful whether General Carteaux gave them more than a casual glance.

> Your arrival, my dear fellow, is welcome but quite unnecessary. We shall be in Toulon tomorrow or the day after. The bayonets of our valient Peoples' Army will see to that. However, you will be able to share in a victory without discomfort or danger. Please stay to dinner.

26

But Toulon was not to fall as Marseille had fallen. Months were to pass before the city and its extensive harbour came once more under the control of the French Government. Carteaux was to have two successors before the plan put forward by Captain Buonaparte of the artillery was accepted and acted upon.

'Toulon will be child's play.' With some such words Carteaux dismissed the subject of military operations and turned to the more pleasant subject of dinner, inviting his guest to sit beside him, which was well, for although some thirty officers were assembled in the mess only those in the immediate vicinity of the general had more than a meagre share of the food and wine. Buonaparte, new to a headquarters mess, was surprised at the favour enjoyed by the top table. He had learned to be a soldier; he had still to learn that '*égalité*' and '*fraternité*' were words thrown out by the powerful to the ignorant, that leaders in social upheavals fatten, while the led must be content to applaud.

Meanwhile professional skill, industry, devotion to duty were as the air Captain Buonaparte breathed, and next morning, whether Toulon was about to succumb to revolutionary bayonets or not, accompanied by General Carteaux in resplendent uniform (Carteaux always shone in scarlet and gold) and his aide-de-camp, Dupas, he set off from Ollioules to inspect the nearest battery which was in position at Montauban, about one kilometre along the road to Toulon.

After listening to some empty talk about where to heat cannon balls before firing them to set fire to British ships in the harbour Buonaparte cut in with the suggestion that a ranging shot first be tried. A shot was accordingly fired and it fell less than a third of the way to the harbour, let alone to the ships. Carteaux turned to his ADC with raised eyebrows. Young Dupas could offer no help, but agreed that the fault lay with the royalists, who, during their temporary control of the Marseille arsenal must have tampered with the powder manufactured there. Buonaparte was prevented from expressing his own views by the arrival on the scene of the two Commissioners, Saliceti and Gaspari, to whom, when Carteaux and Dupas were out of hearing, he whispered his exasperation. How could any military operation succeed when directed by such self-satisfied ignorance? The enthusiasm of amateurs might well overcome civil disobedience in Avignon or Marseille; far more was needed to defeat the organized power of an invading force of British and Spanish regular troops, backed up by a powerful fleet.

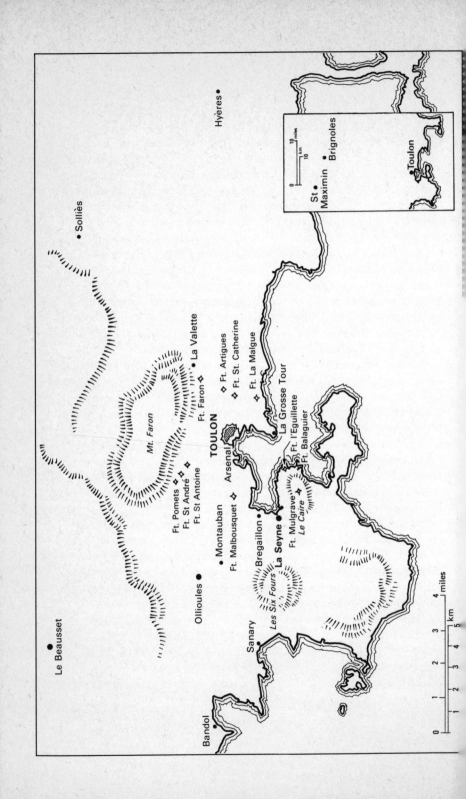

Nevertheless, for as long as he, Buonaparte, had the ear and the approval of the Commissioners the situation was hopeful. Luck, too, favoured him, for he owed his appointment not to the War Office but to the more influential local Representatives of the People. Still better luck was in store. It could not have been known at the time but within a few weeks Saliceti and Gaspari were to be joined as Commissioners by Augustin Robespierre, brother of the dictator though fortunately less fanatical. From then on communication between the commander of the artillery of the army besieging Toulon and the Committee of Public Safety could not have been closer. Buonaparte, in modern terms, was on a direct line to the Government. Such disapproval or jealousy as the Army Commander might have felt at this threat to his authority would have had to simmer beneath a tightly screwed lid. General Carteaux was in any case far too flattered by his exalted position, his gold braid and his weakness for good food and wine, to exhibit any greater resentment than to nickname his newly arrived artillery commander Captain Canon.

The land defences of Toulon included a ring of forts: those on the west, which were to play an important role during the coming weeks, were Malbousquet and Mulgrave; nearer the harbour entrance were Eguillette and Balaguier. Opposite across the water was La Grosse Tour. A short distance south-west of Montauban, where Carteaux's ineffective battery of guns had taken up position, was the hill of Les Six Fours, the highest point in the district, dominating La Seyne, then a fishing village at the water's edge, now a great arsenal, situated just over two kilometres due west of Eguillette, at the far end of an inlet from the harbour. Today Les Six Fours is crowned by a naval fort into which strangers may penetrate only when armed with a pass signed by the Admiral commanding Toulon. Where the fort now stands Captain Buonaparte stood to make a reconnaissance of the area. No place could be better. From that hilltop the view is extensive, its beauty impressive. On a clear day one can see the Mediterranean coast eastward to Hyères, westward to the wide sweep of the bay enclosing Sanary and Bandol and far beyond towards Marseille.

But it was not to admire scenic beauty that Captain Buonaparte stood there on the morning after taking up his command. His object was to examine the defences of Toulon and assess their strategic value. He could see the city and beyond it the heights which gave such secure protection from attack by land, the highest being the Faron, covering the approach from the north. Less formidable hills stretch eastward to Sollies and La Valette, the village where the Buonaparte family had found refuge on arriving from Corsica three months before. To the west is the gap along which General Carteaux's troops had made a limited advance. Assault from the land would be difficult and costly. It would demand careful preparation and the use of large forces. It could easily develop into a long siege, and the Committee of Public Safety had no time to lose. Royalist rebellion, especially when aided by foreign enemies, must be crushed before it crushed the Committee.

Far below, Buonaparte could see the vast outer harbour and the smaller though still extensive inner harbour where enemy ships rode at anchor. Eguillette was out of sight, hidden below the hill of Le Caire, but Fort Balaguier, a short distance to its right, and the Grosse Tour on the far side of that surprisingly narrow entrance – some fifteen hundred metres only – were clearly visible.

The area was already familiar to Buonaparte, several of his journeys to and from Corsica having taken him to Toulon. On these occasions the harbour entrance had held no special significance for him and the tricolour had fluttered from the guardian forts bidding welcome to French mariners. Now all was changed. British and Spanish troops manned the defences and in the city itself the British flag had been hoisted, to the alarm of the French royalists who would have preferred the Fleur de Lys. Was not Louis XVII now King of France? Strong allies were welcome but they must not be too strong. The English in particular were guests who were apt to overstay their welcome.

The key to Toulon was the narrow entrance to the outer harbour. He who held that key could turn it as in a lock. Bring the entrance under effective fire and unfriendly ships within the harbour must either beat a hasty retreat out to sea or face destruction. There would be no need for a general infantry attack, except as a diversion. The solution was bombardment of the defences of the low hill of Le Caire, followed by a spirited attack up to the summit and on down the slope leading to the water's edge where stood Fort Eguillette. The Fort would be taken in reverse, for its guns were, of course, sited to fire outwards over the harbour.

It needed only a few seconds for these thoughts to pass through Captain Buonaparte's mind as he gazed eastward from the summit of

Les Six Fours; it took even less for a decision to follow. The plan was so simple and seems so obvious to the visitor standing today where Buonaparte stood a hundred and eighty years ago, that he can but ask himself: Why did nobody else think of it? And why, once put forward, was it not immediately adopted?

The fort, constructed in later years on the crest of Le Caire, and which aptly bears the name Fort Napoleon, does not provide an answer to these questions; it records what is of more value: the first step of a military genius into the limelight.

Captain Buonaparte remounted his horse and rode down the hill again to army HQ at Ollioules, four kilometres to the north.

From the first it was apparent that both Saliceti and Gaspari were on Buonaparte's side, not only because he was a fellow Corsican but because it was clear to them that he was a professional among amateurs and far and away the most intelligent officer in the region. If success was to come and, Commissioners or not, their lives depended on it, it could only come through him. Some weeks were to pass before they were able to convert others, more highly placed, to their view, or to the fact that General Carteaux must go. This was not easy, for Carteaux had friends at court.

Meanwhile Captain Buonaparte set to work with inexhaustible energy. On 17 September, ten days after his interview with Saliceti at Le Beausset, he received official confirmation of his appointment. His promotion to the rank of major followed. But he had not waited on events. On the day after his visit with Carteaux to that battery of guns sited at such a harmless distance from the enemy, he ordered it forward to Brégaillon at the head of an inlet from the harbour, just north of La Seyne which was still in enemy hands. From Brégaillon the range was still too great seriously to threaten the coming and going of ships, but they were at least forced to keep their distance. The move might have alerted the allied command to the dangerous situation which must ensue if the French continued their advance, but little notice was taken of it. Perhaps the defences of La Seyne and Le Caire were thought to be sufficiently strong. A more serious threat was needed, and it was not long in coming.

Upon the insistance of his artillery commander General Carteaux reluctantly agreed to an attack being made on Le Caire. Something had to be done to keep this hot-headed young man quiet. Also the

Commissioners might become unhappy if their favourite was ignored. The attack was, however, sanctioned with so little grace, was so ill-prepared and performed with so little enthusiasm that failure was inevitable. The only result, apart from a small loss of life, was to alarm the Allies, this time seriously. Reinforcements were promptly landed at Eguillette. Fort Mulgrave, crowning the hill of Le Caire, was strengthened, and General O'Hara, Governor of Toulon and commander of all land forces, arrived in person to take charge. The armament was increased by twenty heavy guns and four mortars, an adequate trench system was constructed and communications improved. To emphasize the change the French gave Fort Mulgrave a new name: Le Petit Gibraltar.

The chance of a quick solution had been missed. Siege warfare must follow and, in fact, three months were to pass before Toulon was returned to its owners. But Capitaine Canon neither abandoned nor altered the plan which he knew to be right. He proceeded with redoubled energy to amass guns and gunners from any and every source within reach. Surprise was no longer enough; increased armament was essential; gun power alone would ensure success.

The Army of the South, in common with other European armies of the day, looked upon artillery mainly as a support for the infantry which, as everybody knew, had all the real work to do. Indeed a parallel may be drawn between the use of guns in the late eighteenth century and the use of tanks in the early part of the twentieth. Both were mistakenly employed in small units, even individually, in support of attacking infantry, instead of as an avalanche of power destined to crush all before it and break the enemy's line.

When Captain Buonaparte joined the Army of the South he found as artillery thirty-one guns of small calibre, two 10-inch mortars and a totally inadequate supply of ammunition, most of it of the wrong size. He wrote directly to the Committee of Public Safety:

> As soon as we are masters of Eguillette and Balaguier we will set up batteries there which will force the enemy to evacuate both harbours. But this will need a considerable siege train. It is artillery that reduces fortresses, making possible the advance of infantry to take possession. It is with great regret that I find little attention has been given to this important matter ... There is no capable officer in charge of the arsenal at Marseille and sound knowledge is essential in whoever

occupies that post. The most important task in gunnery is the formation of a siege train. The artillery was not organized at all when I joined this army. Now, thanks to the orders you have issued, things are beginning to move. I have had to struggle against ignorance and the passions it gives rise to ... The first step I propose is that you should send to command the artillery a general who can, if only by seniority of rank, ensure respect and deal with a crowd of fools on the staff with whom one has constantly to argue, lay down the law in order to overcome their prejudice and force them to act in a manner which theory and practice alike have shown to be axiomatic to any trained officer of this corps.

This letter was dated 25 October 1793 and signed: 'Buonaparte, Commanding the Artillery, Army of the South'.

'The fools on the staff' – the refrain has been heard since armies existed, but not the suggestion that a senior officer should be appointed to control both fools and the author of the suggestion, more especially when the author is a youth of twenty-four and has held his command for just over five weeks. One may imagine the feelings of the Chief of the General Staff in Whitehall at finding such a letter on his desk – if it ever got there! But in days of revolution anything can happen. What Carnot, Minister of War, or Bouchotte, his assistant, thought we cannot know, but it would no doubt be sufficient for them that the officer commanding the artillery of the Army of the South had the approval of the Commissioners. That is what the Commissioners were for: to keep an eye on the conduct of generals and to ensure full and accurate information reaching the Goverment.

When the War Office received, a few days after the letter, another from Commissioner Saliceti which read: 'Buonaparte is the only officer with the right ideas,' direct reports from the artillery commander were not only read with added interest but the question was asked: What has gone wrong with General Carteaux?

Robespierre himself must have heard praise of the new arrival at the headquarters of the Army of the South and have been impressed, for during that autumn he offered Buonaparte the command of the Paris section of the National Guard, but he refused it, preferring, as any regular officer would, to face outward to the enemy beyond the frontier rather than inward with the risk of opening fire on his own countrymen. Less than a year later he no doubt blessed this wise decision, for in the following July the commander of the Paris National

33

Guard, Hanriot, followed Robespierre to the guillotine.

Meanwhile, though Buonaparte might refuse a command at the centre of power, power came to him; for the dictator's younger brother, Augustin Robespierre, arriving at Ollioules, immediately became his friend and admirer. From then on contact with the dictator himself was close and continuous, though in fact the soldier did not actively seek it, being wholly occupied with the work in hand. Within a month he had increased the number of guns to over a hundred, some of them long range mortars destined for the bombardment of Toulon, should that become necessary. His energy was untiring, his demands relentless. 'We must procure horses for the artillery park. Requisition enough horses to form four brigades. I want three hundred animals.' This was part of a letter to Major Gassendi, a gunner friend who had been brought over from the Army of Italy, now being stripped of its equipment in favour of that besieging Toulon. As usual it was Saliceti who had arranged the transfer. The letter continues:

> You are by now, I expect, in Grenoble. One of the things we need most is 8,000 to 10,000 spare muskets. You will be going to Saint Etienne so you will easily manage to have these sent to us. I have not been able to procure as many pioneer tools as I had hoped. See if you can get some in Grenoble or Valence. What we mainly lack are axes and spades. I am not sending you the original order of the Representatives of the People (an order for Gassendi's posting), as I have sent the certified copy to the Minister, and I need to retain the original myself.

When this letter to Major Gassendi was despatched on 4 November Carteaux had already handed over his command to General Doppet. It had become clear to all that Carteaux must go, his departure being hastened by such recommendations to his artillery commander as 'Make sure the wind is blowing in the right direction before you open fire'.

Yet even now Saliceti and Gaspari must walk with care. As though fearing to act on their own they invoked the help of Commissioners Barras and Fréron, recently freed from their duty of converting the citizens of Marseille to the way of truth. Augustin Robespierre, having just arrived at Ollioules, was added to the list, and the five, meeting in Le Beausset on 12 October, decided unanimously on Carteaux's dismissal. Yet even now they took precautions. Getting rid of a general in 1793 was one thing, getting rid of a Jacobin general another, a distinction which may be compared in certain countries today with dismissing an ordinary general and a general who is a member of 'the Party'. Then, as now, generals and others highly placed could be dismissed by the method known as 'kicking upstairs'. Carteaux was kicked sideways, and landed unhurt in the Army of Italy, engaged in occupying Nice, which only a few months before had been annexed by France and had accepted its fate without resentment. There, since nothing was happening, General Carteaux could do no harm. Honour unsullied, his reputation only slightly dimmed, accompanied by young Dupas, he would be free to ride across the sunlit hills, perhaps stand at La Turbie in contemplation of the memorial to the Roman warriors with whom he had so little in common, or, according to whim, swim in the warm waters of the Mediterranean. Waited on by fraternal though far from equal *citoyens de la Republique*, he would have leisure to indulge his appetite for good food and wine in a land where both abound. Kicked sideways into the happy surroundings of Provence General Carteaux fades from history.

The new general, Doppet, was brought down from Lyon where Citizen Fouché, destined in later years to become Napoleon's Chief of Police, was engaged in punishing rebellious citizens with *une sévérité inéxorable*. General Doppet was a better choice than Carteaux, but only just. Before the Revolution he had been a physician. Then politics drew him and he became an enthusiastic member of his local Jacobin Club. Like Carteaux he found favour with men in power and like him became a general. Without knowledge, training or experience, he now found himself in command of an important theatre of operations. As a man Doppet had much in his favour. He was more intelligent and less of a clown than Carteaux, kinder, humbler, more sensitive – too sensitive for the cruelty of battle, as will be seen. In his favour, too, was his instant appreciation of talent in others, in particular his admiration of the qualities of his artillery commander.

> Every time I went to inspect the line I found him at his post. He slept on the ground wrapped in his cloak. He never left his guns.

This was General Doppet's written opinion of Major Buonaparte. Could any officer of any army wish for higher praise? But despite Doppet's clear-sighted opinion and his full approval of Buonaparte's plan of attack, his period of command was brief, a mere three weeks. It was brought to an end by a sudden, undisciplined, unprepared attack on the hill of Le Caire by part of the Regiment of the Côte d'Or. Men on duty in a front-line trench – from where in those days a man could look over the top with little risk, the musket having nothing of the precision or the range of a modern sniper's rifle – saw, or thought they saw, Spanish troops ill-treating French prisoners. With generous ardour and French *élan* they rushed forward to rescue and avenge their comrades. Other troops joined in and the action became general. Bored by inactivity, glad of an opportunity for action, their officers powerless to restrain them, the Revolutionary soldiers of France, always without discipline, staged a miniature battle which could only end to their disadvantage.

Buonaparte never far from the enemy, cried to Doppet: 'The wine is uncorked, it must be drunk,' and ran to join the attackers.

It is doubtful whether such a scatterbrained attack could have dislodged the Allies from Le Caire and captured the all-important Eguillette, the garrison having, as we know, been heavily reinforced, guns sited to command all approach from the west, and communications with the rear improved. All doubt was, however, effectively removed by General Doppet, who, shocked by seeing an officer at his side cut in two by a cannon ball, ordered the cease-fire to be sounded. French exuberance having by that time gone off the boil, the order was quickly, perhaps gratefully, obeyed. The men retired to their trenches, the firing died down and order was restored.

It has been said that Buonaparte, when the cease-fire sounded, cried out within hearing of General Doppet, 'The fool who called off the action has robbed us of Toulon.' Strong words which might well have been said in a moment of excitement and disappointment, but scarcely within the hearing of a commanding general. What is more credible is that in the hours following the abortive attack Major Buonaparte recounted in detail the various happenings to the two Commissioners; for Doppet was removed from his command on the next day and transferred to the Army of the Pyrenees, which, like the Army of Italy, was not engaged in operations. The Committee of Public Safety – fortunately for dismissed generals – had at its disposal a selection of armies where they could be harmlessly employed.

Inefficient generals were invariably not sent back to Paris in disgrace, with a trial and execution looming in the background. Perhaps loyalty to revolutionary ideals, endorsement of the practice of terror, atoned for professional incompetence? Or was it that exceptional kindness was extended to members of the extreme left? There again, leaders of experience were not easy to find, for as terror grew so did emigration.

As though determined to avoid further trouble at Toulon the Committee now chose a soldier of long service and undoubted merit – General Dugommier. Known in pre-revolutionary days as Coquille Du Gommier, he was now fifty-five and had seen service in America. He was courageous, intelligent, broad-minded and willing to recognize talent in others. Unfortunately he lacked good health. The Commissioners received him at Ollioules with guarded words and made no secret of the fact that it was now or never. Toulon must be taken or else! The threat, however, was unnecessary for no sooner had Dugommier assumed command in mid-November than he became convinced that his artillery officer had the right answer, and he proceeded to give him full support. From now on all was plain sailing – as far as anything can be in war.

To improve the situation, Buonaparte's request that a senior artillery general be appointed was answered at the same time by the appearance of General Jean du Teil, who reserved for him the same admiration his brother had expressed some years ago at Auxonne. From now on Major Buonaparte was not only allowed freedom to act but encouraged at every turn.

The two generals were both advanced in years, perhaps old-fashioned. Du Teil in particular was afflicted with gout. It is to their credit that they held the reins with light hands, allowing dynamic youth to lead on at a gallop. Experience combined with youthful genius must and did result in success. At long last the Army of the South was marching in step along the right road. The members of the Committee of Public Safety need worry no longer – except to look over their shoulders. But they were accustomed to that.

Chapter 7

Battle

On the day after Dugommier's arrival Buonaparte sent a detailed draft of his plan for the reduction of Toulon to the Committee of Public Safety. Several weeks before this Commissioner Saliceti had added his personal recommendation to an outline of the same plan, but Paris was either too busy or too hesitant, and delayed its approval of the plan until the end of November, by which time it was superfluous, for by then those on the spot had taken things into their own hands and had decided upon action.

Here, then, is the plan, or more precisely a letter reminding the Government of its existence.

To Citizen Bouchotte   Army Headquarters
Ministry of War   Ollioules
                                               4 November 1793

Citizen Minister
The plan which I have laid before the commanding generals and the representatives of the people is, I believe, the only practicable one. If it had been adopted from the beginning with a little more warmth it is probable we should now be in Toulon.

To drive the enemy from the harbour is the first consideration, and to become masters of the harbour we must seize the promontory of Eguillette. Subsequently it is possible that, surprised by this move and fearing to lose control of the harbour the enemy will decide upon retreat.

You will realize that this is hypothetical. A month ago, before the enemy received reinforcements, it would have been certain. It is, of course, possible that the garrison might hold out and stand a siege, even if the fleet were forced to evacuate the roads. In that case the two batteries established opposite Malbousquet would be immediately reinforced by a third and the mortars – which would have been bombarding Toulon for three days – would be turned on Malbousquet. That fort could not hold out more than forty-eight hours and afterwards there would be nothing to prevent us reaching the walls of Toulon. These we assault at the Marais and Arsenal bastions, and, covered by the guns at Malbousquet and those on the slopes of the Arenes, we reach the second line. During this operation we should be under fire from Fort Artigues but the four mortars and the six guns already brought to bear on it would still be in position and would continue their fire.

To undertake this last stage of the siege it is essential that the items requested in the attached inventory shall be made available for our artillery park.

It is more than a month since I told the generals that our existing artillery was inadequate to silence fire from the English redoubt on the promontory overlooking Eguillette.

There have been other instances of competence in a youthful mind, there can never have been one more convincing. Who in the Paris War Office in the autumn of 1793 could fail to respond to the intellectual clarity, the maturity of judgement of this young artillery officer, and think when putting down the letter: 'Here is our man'?

The generals referred to by Buonaparte, it need hardly be said, included neither Dugommier nor du Teil, for not only were both ready to accept his ideas 'with a little more warmth' but to fan them to flame.

Before a reply had been received from Paris a Council of War was held at Le Beausset. General Dugommier presided and Buonaparte acted as secretary, recording the proceedings in his usual illegible scrawl (his writing could never keep pace with his thoughts) but with undoubted accuracy; for it was his own plan that was at last to be put into operation, with or without the approval of the War Office.

All senior officers in the region were present: General du Teil, Major-Generals Lapoype and Mouret, seven other members of the Headquarter Staff, and of course the Commissioners Saliceti and Gaspari. It was decided that after a three-day bombardment a dawn attack would be launched against Le Caire – Little Gibraltar. Once the defences erected by the Allies on the summit were in French hands the advance would continue downhill to Eguillette and Balaguier, and batteries would then be brought forward to command the entrance to the harbour. The two forts were strongly built with underground casemates and protected gun emplacements, but their armament pointed seawards and they would be vulnerable to an attack from the land in their rear. Also they were of ancient construction, Eguillette dating from 1672 and Balaguier from a few years earlier when Vauban was ringing France with what were then the last word in fortifications. Both stand today as they have stood through the centuries, one a store for naval equipment, the other a museum in name only, its large empty rooms now silent.

On the other side of the harbour entrance is La Tour Royale of far older construction. But Buonaparte's plan was not concerned with this. General Lapoype, who had had his say at that meeting at Le Beausset, commanded, somewhat surprisingly, an entirely independent force also due to attack Toulon, but from the north and east. To date his men had not been seriously engaged. Now they would make a diversionary attack on Mount Faron while the real business was taking place in the west.

Lapoype's small army was reinforced before the day of action by an infantry brigade under the command of a soldier since famous, André Masséna. At the age of seventeen, long before the Revolution had thrown open the door to promotion, Masséna had left his village home at Levens, not far from Nice, and had enlisted in the ranks. He was now thirty-eight and a Brigadier-General. He had probably never heard of the young major commanding the artillery of the army on the other side of the harbour. But the major would very soon overtake him with giant strides and later create him a Marshal of France, Prince d'Essling and Duc de Rivoli. The Army would christen him *Enfant chéri de la Victoire*. Today in Provence and elsewhere parks, squares and avenues keep alive his memory.

Another figure that enters upon the Napoleonic scene at Toulon is that of Andoche Junot, at the time a youthful sergeant but destined to rise in rank and to serve Napoleon with unswerving devotion through the years. At Toulon, Major Buonaparte, having discovered that Sergeant Junot could write legibly, employed him as secretary and dictated orders to him. After success at Toulon Junot was promoted to the rank of captain and became Aide-de-Camp to his hero. He was brave, loyal, vain and stupid. He became a general but never a marshal. By way of compensation Napoleon created him Duc d'Abrantes. He died sadly and tragically by his own hand two years before his master met disaster at Waterloo.

It might seem, in contrast to the nervous activity of the French – their repeated changes of command, order and counter-order, planning and replanning, correspondence with Paris and impatient waiting for the decisions of men far removed from the scene of action – that the British and Spanish troops were inactive. Their objective was, of course, different. To obtain a decision the French must attack, the allies need only stubbornly defend what they had seized. To venture out of their trenches and attempt to drive the French back into their own country would be courting disaster; it was a long way to Paris.

However on 30 November, having learnt of the decision made at Le Beausset, General O'Hara attacked in order to delay or disrupt French preparations. This attack, which surprised the French, was at first successful. French guns were captured and at one moment it looked as if Dugommier's Headquarters at Ollioules would be overrun. The allied troops were forced back by a spirited counter-attack organized and led personally by Major Buonaparte, determined to restore the situation and save his guns. Though praised by his previous commander, General Doppet, for never leaving his guns, he did at times leave them – but only in the direction of the enemy. And now a party of infantry led by him along a concealed trench came suddenly upon the flank of a British regiment and opened fire at close range. An officer, standing exposed on the parapet, was wounded and fell forward towards the French. Buonaparte made him his prisoner and generously returned him his sword. The officer was General O'Hara.

A week after the British attack Buonaparte wrote to his friend Gassendi:

> Here things are much as usual. The Army now numbers 30,000 and we have eleven batteries trained on Fort Malbousquet and the defences of Eguillette. A few days ago the enemy attacked and tried to capture the important battery of the Convention which consists of seven 24-pounders. They seized the guns and spiked them but were later thrown back. We took two hundred prisoners, including General

O'Hara, a Spanish colonel, an English major, and about twenty other officers. The action lasted seven hours. We lost some fifty killed and a hundred and fifty wounded.

Thus ended Buonaparte's first battle. It was to be followed two weeks later by his second, which resulted in the fall of Toulon. Both were but a minor prelude to the thunderous symphony of sixty battles he was to fight in the next twenty-two years, winning all but two of them. Alas, to what effect? Their sound has long since died away, nothing remains of their unsubstantial glory but a row of tattered flags hanging from the walls of the chapel in the Invalides. Generals who feared him, staff-officers, aides-de-camp to whom he was a god, found death at his side; nineteen horses were shot under him. He remained untouched save for two minor wounds: the thrust of a British bayonet and a bullet in the heel. But here, at Toulon, he was still the young soldier, splendid in leadership and courage. Ambition had not yet blinded, power had not yet corrupted him.

17 December had been chosen as the day for the French attack, which was preceded by a heavy bombardment of the enemy position. On the night before the attack a storm broke over Toulon and torrential rain fell. The Command hesitated; even the Commissioners were for calling it off. Buonaparte, however, brushed aside amateur fears with professional reasoning; the same rain was falling on the defenders; it would hinder them as much or more than the attackers; it might lead them to think that no attack would be possible, in which case surprise would be greater. In any case it was too late now to warn Lapoype away on the other side of Toulon; he would be left to carry out his diversionary attack unsupported. The attack took place as planned.

Again we hear of Major Buonaparte leaving his guns, this time accompanied by another officer of the same arm, Muiron, who was commanding the right wing of the attack. Side by side, swords in hand, the two led an infantry battalion against a crucial point at a crucial moment. Buonaparte was wounded in the calf by a British bayonet. A certain Hernandez bound up the wound, which was not serious, and he continued in action and accompanied the troops in the storming of the hill of Le Caire. The ragged, undisciplined, but brave, soldiers of Revolutionary France climbed the hill, the drums beating out the *Ça Ira*, officers and men crying '*Vive La République*', as, in the years to come, they would cry '*Vive L'Empereur*'.

The crest of the hill in their hands, the French continued their advance down to the water's edge, where the two forts were occupied without opposition, the allies having decided to evacuate them and withdraw the garrisons to the ships. Food, stores and ammunition had been left in quantity; nor had there been time to spike the guns. Captain Marmont, one day to become a marshal of France, took over command of the captured position.

The allied intention had been that Fort Malbousquet, overlooking the harbour farther north, should hold out and cover the retreat from La Seyne, in fact from the whole area, but this fort also fell to a French assault, making total evacuation of the British and Spanish forces imperative.

When the rain ceased and the sun shone again over Toulon harbour it shone too on a happy Buonaparte who stood surveying the scene from the hilltop where now stands Fort Napoleon. Victory was not yet complete, but it was near. When news came that Lapoype and Masséna had captured Le Faron and were approaching the city it was nearer still. Triumph followed on the afternoon of the next day when French guns were in position at Eguillette and Balaguier and the combined fleets were seen making sail and moving out to sea.

The hill of Le Caire may be climbed today, for by chance, except for the growth of trees, it has remained unchanged since Major Buonaparte and his men climbed it, drenched to the skin, in the dawn of a December day more than one hundred and eighty years ago. It rises in a military zone to be entered only by permission of the army command in Toulon, and in the company of an officer. One climbs the slope through tangled undergrowth, or alternatively drives up a narrow winding road leading finally to the gate of Fort Napoleon. There one may stand as Napoleon stood in the hour of victory, gazing down to the harbour from which enemy warships were sailing in slow procession, the White Ensign or the flag of Spain fluttering from mastheads. It must have been a great moment for one so young. On 24 December Buonaparte wrote to Citizen Dupin, Assistant Minister of War, 'I promised you success and, as you see, I have kept my promise.'

Chapter 8

After battle

Those French royalists of Toulon for whom room could be found on the warships were taken on board and afterwards landed at Elba or on the coast of Italy. The many who remained on the quay watched with dismay and growing fear the departure of the fleet. On the morning of 19 December the Revolutionary Army entered Toulon. Cheering crowds filled the streets, and men who for three months had dreamed they had a king hurried into hiding or bravely awaited their fate at the hands of Commissioners Barras and Fréron, who were soon able to report that all naval officers who had gone over to the British when Lord Hood entered the harbour had been shot. A guillotine was erected in the square. Twelve thousand workmen were employed in pulling down monuments and public buildings. 'Infamous' Toulon was re-named Port-of-the-Mountain.

Fouché, hurrying to Toulon from Lyon where he had assisted in restoring order with his usual *sévérité inéxorable*, wrote to a fellow member of the National Convention: 'We are celebrating the victory this evening by killing off two hundred and sixteen rebels. *Au-revoir*, my friend. My eyes fill with tears of joy, happiness overflows in my heart.' How touching. In our own day a Stalin could not have expressed more delicate feelings.

Captain Marmont, a more desirable witness, told of the inhabitants being assembled in the square and encouraged to point out any of their number suspected of being enemies of the Republic, whereupon the more quick-witted, sensing which way the wind was blowing, and hoping to escape its cruel blast, loudly accused the nearest personal enemy or the nearest creditor. The victim was then taken away and shot. It is to be hoped that Marmont exaggerated what happened in Toulon in December 1793.

Meanwhile General du Teil, Buonaparte's immediate superior, whose activities were confined to the field of battle, where honour reigns over vengeance, reported to his superiors, 'I find difficulty in doing justice to Major Buonaparte's many qualities. Sound knowledge, keen intelligence, if anything, too much courage.' Better still, and in the circumstances more important, was the decision Commissioners Saliceti and Gaspari made immediately after the fall of Toulon: 'The Representatives of the People, bearing in mind the zeal and intelligence of which Citizen Buonaparte has given proof, have decided to recommend his promotion to the rank of Brigadier-General.'

It was not unusual at the time for an officer to achieve rapid promotion; many had done so, and as many had fallen even more rapidly. During the first four years of The Revolution army generals had been dismissed at the average yearly rate of one hundred and seventy, and in the case of at least half that number dismissal meant not only the end of a career but of life. As far as the Government was concerned this more drastic method of ridding itself of those who incurred its displeasure had the double advantage of silencing argument and reducing expense at one stroke.

For the moment Buonaparte need not fear an adverse report; Saliceti was his admirer, Augustin Robespierre his friend. Meanwhile promotion meant not only recognition of merit but a substantial increase of pay. Letitzia, who with her five younger children had lived for the last six months in a Marseille slum dependent on state aid to refugees and such small sums as her soldier son could spare from his pay, could now look to the future with more confidence.

Joseph, Lucien and Uncle Fesch, each of whom had been found employment by Saliceti, may or may not have followed the example of Napoleon, who, from the day he began to earn money had deprived himself of what others considered essential in order to help his mother. Joseph had been early to Paris to stake a claim for the family against the sum voted by the Convention for the assistance of Corsican refugees. Afterwards his kind, indolent nature did not encourage hard work and he went to join his mother and his sisters in Marseille. There dull Julie Clary, daughter of a prosperous merchant, accepted his offer of marriage and brought with her a substantial dowry of some twenty thousand francs, a generous sum in the late eighteenth century. His brother, inspecting gun positions along the coast, found time to say, 'Lucky dog, Joseph'. But Joseph, though impecunious and unemployed, could still offer advantages to the Clary family. He had indeed, no doubt through the influence of Saliceti, saved one of its members from arrest and imprisonment as an enemy of the Republic. Monsieur and Madame Clary also knew that Joseph's brother was not only a coming general but an intimate friend of Robespierre's brother. As the years passed the Clary family had further cause to congratulate themselves on the marriage, for their Julie was to be twice a queen.

Though without personality or pleasing features herself, Julie had a younger sister, Désirée, who possessed both. General Buonaparte, visiting Marseille occasionally during the spring and summer of 1794, made her acquaintance, admired her and among the first of his invasions was that of her bedroom. However, when he asked for her hand in marriage, it was refused him. 'One Buonaparte in the family is enough,' said Madame Clary.

Yet Desirée was not to escape entirely; Bernadotte, Marshal of France and afterwards King of Sweden, married her, though she chose to reside in France rather than grace the Swedish throne. The Clary family, like the Buonapartes, were among the fortunate, or unfortunate, destined to be plucked by fate from the blurred mass of humanity and placed upon a pinnacle for all the world to see.

Lucien-Brutus was still at Saint Maximin, some twenty miles inland, where he handed out stores, though without enthusiasm, his heart being in politics. He had been elected President of the local Jacobin Club, where with impassioned eloquence he sought to convince a gaping peasantry that earthly happiness and prosperity were to be found only in a France freed from the tyranny of kings and the greed of nobles, that in future the Committee of Public Safety would voice the will of God, or in His absence that of Robespierre. Lucien-Brutus fell in love with his landlord's niece, Catherine Boyer, plump, plain, illiterate and marked by smallpox, but whose moral qualities outweighed all such defects. Lucien, although highly intelligent, was not physically attractive: he had a small head and long spidery arms and legs; he was

46

also short-sighted which caused him to be constantly screwing up his eyes in order to bring his surroundings into focus. He and Catherine were married on 4 May 1794. She was twenty-one, he eighteen, though to avoid having to produce parental consent he added three years to his age. 'I have met a girl who is poor and virtuous and I have married her.' This was the first Madame Mère knew of the marriage and the news hurt and angered her. The law forbade the marriage of minors without the consent of their parents, but, the law apart, Lucien's sense of filial duty, or even of common courtesy, might have prompted him at least to inform his mother of his intended marriage. This was not the last such disappointment Letitzia Buonaparte was to experience. Two years later, Napoleon, on whom she counted more than all the others, also married without her knowledge or consent, and to a woman of questionable conduct, to say the least. However, when Letitzia came to know Catherine she immediately appreciated her simple, loyal nature and her capacity for making her husband happy. This was hardly the case when Napoleon introduced his wife to the family; she was received with frigid disapproval. Napoleon strongly disapproved of his younger brother's marriage. This was no time for the family to welcome union with a penniless peasant. They were about to soar away from such entanglements. Lucien did not seem to understand that they were on the way up.

This was only the first time that Lucien rebelled against his brother's iron will. As the years passed it became a habit. Alone in the Buonaparte family he went his own way and took the consequences. No throne for Lucien. He had to content himself with becoming Prince of Canino, an Italian town of some three thousand inhabitants hardly visible on the map. Catherine bore him three children and died after six years of marriage, pregnant of a fourth. Lucien's subsequent conduct, as far as women were concerned, was unworthy of her.

Appointed, immediately after the fall of Toulon, Inspector of Coastal Defences from Marseille to Menton on the Italian frontier, General Buonaparte was able to visit his mother and flirt with Désirée Clary. But his attentions were hurried. His duty, his career as a soldier, absorbed him. Early in January 1794, he writes to Citizen Bouchotte, Minister of War:

> I am far from satisfied with the companies of coastal gunners. They never practice and are as ignorant as on the day they joined. I am

engaged in re-constructing most of the batteries which are at the moment of little use owing to the incompetence of those who have hitherto been in command.

It is a fairly common practice for men appointed to positions of power to criticize their predecessors, hoping thus to cover their own failings. If Buonaparte gave way to the temptation early in his career, his subsequent success absolves him – unless we except the blame he attached to de Grouchy for his defeat at Waterloo. Reporting in February from Marseille to the Committee of Public Safety, he has no words to waste on the past:

> It is urgently necessary to bring order into the accounts of the artillery and the engineers. Important sums are being wasted on very bad work ... I have just come from Martigues [near Marseille]. Previously there were 4 bronze 16-pounders there on solid mountings, but the latter have been changed for marine mountings in the belief that fixed ones are useless. [The Navy had previously been in charge of the coastal batteries.] Another matter needing your attention is the voting of a decree to place the whole organization of coastal gunners on a permanent basis. I have persuaded the Representative of the People to make a temporary ruling. But this is not enough. A definite law is needed. Far too many people are being paid without regard to their service or usefulness.

On the last day of the same month another report is dated from Saint Tropez:

> Since the capture of Toulon I have been occupied in putting our coasts into a respectable state of defence. The bay of Saint Tropez is blockaded by an enemy squadron which intercepts our convoys. They have already captured some ships laden with supplies. In future these convoys will be protected by two batteries which I am having installed. As soon as they are in position I hope that communication between Nice and Marseille will be free from danger ... the whole of this coast is weak in defence. It is deficient of a great many guns ... I leave today to complete my inspection as far as Menton. As soon as I return I will submit a full report showing the purpose of each battery, its previous condition, the improvements that have been effected, the supply situation and that of the gun crews.

Brigadier-General Buonaparte was now installed in a requisitioned house, Château Sallé, at Antibes. His annual pay was 15,000 francs, an excellent step up from the 1,000 francs that he had received as a junior subaltern at Valence. He was allowed rations for six, and three horses. Junot, the sergeant from Toulon, now a captain, was his ADC, and he was assisted by a staff of three, one of whom was Marmont. Both Junot and Marmont were to remain his loyal friends through the years – Junot to the end and beyond, Marmont until 1814, when loyalty to France gave precedence over devotion to an Emperor who had lost all sense of proportion. He had also brought the family over from Marseille to share his quarters and no doubt the six rations. From now on Letitzia, her three girls, Louis and little Jerome, now aged nine, enjoyed pleasanter surroundings.

In days to come the Buonaparte family must have looked back on the spring and summer of 1794 as a time of unclouded happiness. They lived in a comfortable house in a warm, sunny climate. The dark days were past. A new and more hopeful life was before them. Napoleon had gained rapid promotion. Elisa, having been educated among well-bred girls for eight years, would find herself at home in any level of society. Pauline, already attractive, promised amorous grace, beauty and ignorance. Caroline had ambition and intelligence. Louis, now sixteen, would very soon be taken under his brother's wing and commissioned as a 2nd Lieutenant. Jerome was still too young to be moved by anything but hunger, whilst danger or discomfort meant only excitement. Madame Mère for the first time knew a sense of security and could watch her children grow up provided with the necessities of life. The sun of Provence shone and in its warmth they blossomed, as yet free from the weight of crowns or the clinging robes of office.

It was not only in Marseille and Saint Maximin that love was at work; in Antibes, too, it was disturbing the atmosphere. Aide-de-Camp Captain Junot had become infatuated with his General's sister, Pauline, who would not be fourteen until the following October, but was ready, if not eager, to fall in love with almost anybody. However, this time Napoleon was on the spot and immediately put his foot down. To Junot, asking for Pauline's hand, he replied, 'My dear Junot you haven't a penny. Pauline hasn't a penny. Result – nil'. Three years later the frivolous, charming Pauline married General Leclerc, a husband chosen for her by her brother. Junot was destined to marry Laure Permon and make her the Duchess of Abrantès.

Chapter 9

The Army of Italy prepares to move

General Pierre Dumerbion, in command of the Army of Italy during the winter of 1794, was fifty-four years old and had therefore seen nearly all his army service under the *Ancien Régime*. Without any notable feat of arms to his credit, he could nevertheless look back with satisfaction on a moderately successful career, and more especially congratulate himself on having so far come through the years of revolution without mishap. The method he had employed was simple and is still in use in various War Offices or Ministries of Defence today. A colonel or major in charge of this or that department, finding that the hour of decision can no longer be delayed, that there is positively no escape from issuing a definite order, drafts it with care but does not sign it. He first takes it to the brigadier whom he asks to initial it. Armed with this protective shield he returns light-footed to his own office and boldly adds his signature. The method may not lead to dynamic action but it does ensure continuity of employment and nights of peaceful sleep. Dumerbion had employed it with great success and, now in command of an army where danger threatened increasingly, though not always from the direction of the enemy, he continued to be faithful to it. This is not to say that he lacked initiative or the power of decision; it indicates merely that he realized the necessity for caution. In his case of course the brigadier was represented by the Civil Commissioners attached to his headquarters without whose approval he never took a step forward. While many of his friends had emigrated or disappeared, Dumerbion reached the end of his career without mishap and died peacefully in his bed at the age of fifty-seven. He may not have achieved renown, but he had lived wisely.

When, early in the year, an order came from Lazare Carnot, military member of the Committee of Public Safety in Paris, that the Army of Italy was to prepare for a spring offensive against the Austrians and Piedmontese in northern Italy Dumerbion's first reaction was to consult his Commissioners. He was immediately advised to employ Brigadier-General Buonaparte as his artillery commander. The appointment, which took place on 18 March and was in addition to Buonaparte's duties as Inspector of Coastal Defences, was welcomed both by him and by the Army Commander. To the first it meant service in the field, the hope of every ambitious soldier. To the second, the assistance on his staff of an officer already highly thought of in his profession and who was also a close friend of the dictator's brother.

As time passed and he came to know Buonaparte better and appreciate his qualities, Dumerbion said to him: 'My boy, let me have a plan of operations such as you are capable of producing and I will carry it out to the best of my ability.' Such recognition by a superior of the value of a staff-officer thirty years his junior is rare in an army commander. Dumerbion, though not brilliant himself, at least recognized brilliance in others and made use of it. In Napoleon's memoirs he is recorded as having been 'a man of sixty, honest, courageous, well read, but a victim to gout and often bedridden'.

A plan of operation in northern Italy had been clear in Buonaparte's mind before he joined the headquarters of the Army of Italy, though it was to be modified or extended as time passed or events made necessary. In general his idea was to drive a wedge between the enemy forces in Piedmont – the Austrians and the Piedmontese. He would hold off the stronger partner, the Austrians, while defeating the weaker, the Piedmontese. When King Amadaeus III, from his palace in Turin, had been persuaded to sue for peace, communications with France via the Alps would be open; the Army of Italy would be freed from menace in its rear and able at will to turn on the Austrians and drive them back across Tuscany, if necessary to Vienna. But they would of course sue for peace before then. Speed would be an essential part of the operation. This, with modifications, was what was passing in Buonaparte's mind in the spring of 1794 when he joined the Army of

Italy in command of the artillery.

It is at this point that Citizen Turreau made a brief appearance on the scene. Turreau de Lignières, member of the National Convention, knew the right people and had, like other politicians, made full use of them. The result of his efforts was to have himself posted as a Representative of the People at Dumerbion's headquarters. Since Augustin Robespierre and Citizen Ricord were already fulfilling that office satisfactorily Turreau's friends at court must have been quite powerful people. Not that it mattered to Turreau who or how many were the Commissioners watching over General Dumerbion's conduct; his visit to the Riviera had very little to do with the duties of a Commissioner, but quite a lot with the sunshine of the Mediterranean coast. For Citizen Turreau, having just married an attractive young woman called Félicité, had hit upon the idea of spending their honeymoon in a more agreeable climate than that of Paris, all expenses paid.

Arriving in Nice Citizen Turreau soon came into contact with General Buonaparte and it is rumoured, that Madame Turreau had enough honeymoon charm left over to exercise some upon the General. However that may be, the three became friends. Discussing the position of the Army of Italy one day with Turreau, Buonaparte remarked that the only way to get things moving was to prod and pester the Paris authorities until they finally gave instructions which could result in a definite victory over the enemy, not merely a half-hearted move forward into enemy territory. This had, of course, been his method at Toulon and it had succeeded. Why should not Turreau, obviously an important member of the Convention, use his influence? 'Give me an additional ten or fifteen thousand men and I will conquer Italy.' The boast may have startled Turreau at the time, but dining with Buonaparte next day he was given details of the plan and became convinced of its worth. Also at the table was Count de Volney, a man of intelligence who has left a reputation as a philosopher and a writer. Two years later de Volney was in the United States, where, learning that General Buonaparte had been put in command of the Army of Italy, he predicted to friends of George Washington the splendid success which so soon followed.

1 *Napoleon, aged sixteen, drawn by one of his friends*

2   *Napoleon's mother as a young woman*

3 *André Masséna as a Divisional General in 1796 (artist unknown)*

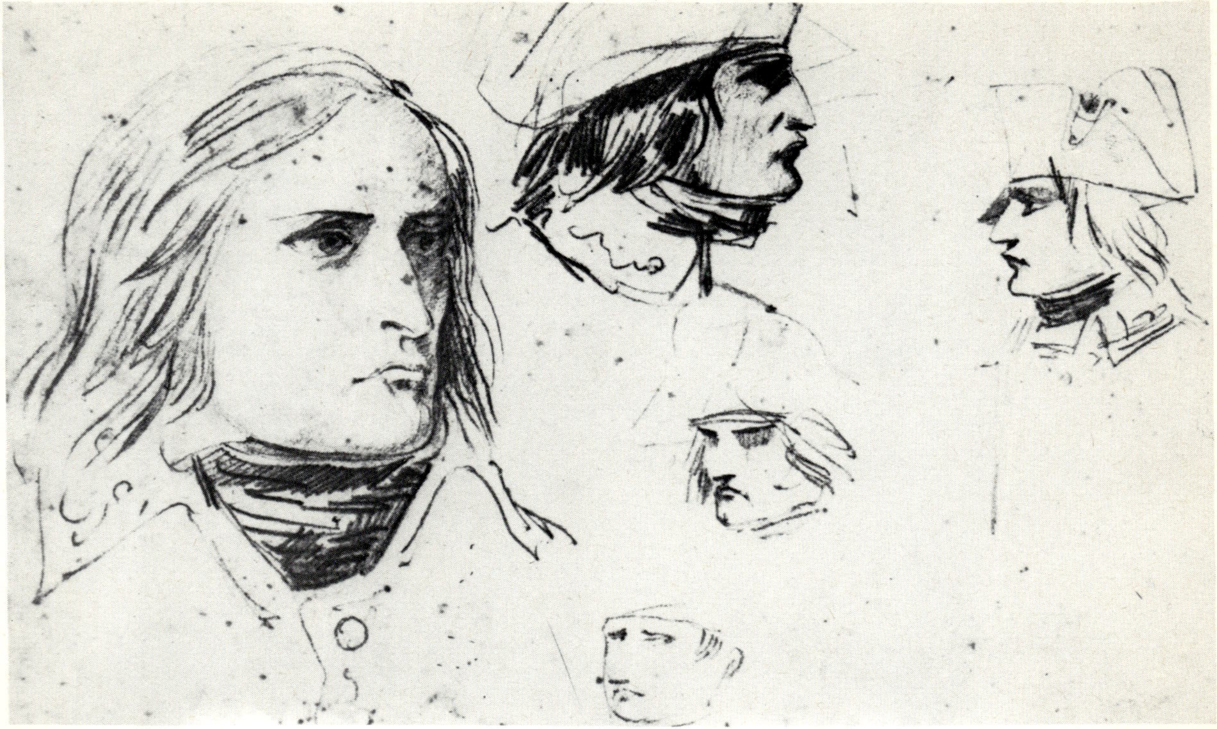

4 *Drawing of Napoleon as a young man, by David*

BUONAPARTE.

Déposé à la Bibl.^e Nat.^{le} le ... an 6 de la Rep.^{que} Franc.^{se}

5   *Buonaparte, aged 25 or 26, drawn by Guerin and deposited in the
      French Bibliothèque Nationale in September 1795*

6   *Christophe Saliceti was a fellow Corsican a few years older than Napoleon. Elected a member of the Revolutionary Government he became a helpful friend to Napoleon's family when they reached France*

7   *Andoche Junot served as a sergeant under Buonaparte at Toulon
and was later his ADC during the Italian Campaign of 1796/7. Though
of modest intellect his courage and unswerving loyalty were rewarded
by the Dukedom of Abrantès*

8　General Buonaparte assuming command of the Army of Italy in Nice on 27 March 1796 at the age of 26. His four divisional commanders are facing him: Masséna aged 38, Sérurier aged 54, Laharpe and Augereau aged 29.

Chapter 10

Rehearsal for a campaign

From March to December 1794, at such times as he was not with the forward troops in Italy General Buonaparte shared the home of the Laurenti family at 1 rue de Villefranche, Nice, where he was close to army HQ and equally well placed to continue his duties as Inspector of Coastal Defences. The address has since been changed to 6 rue Bonaparte but the house remains much as it then was, a dignified, solid, stone-built edifice, though the orchard of orange and lemon trees which once surrounded it has disappeared beneath adjoining masonry.

Count Joseph Laurenti (no doubt known in the fashion of the time as Citizen Laurenti) and his wife had a fine library and an attractive daughter Emilia, aged fifteen. 'How fortunate you are to have so many books,' observed Buonaparte, when being shown round. 'They are yours, General, to use as you wish.' Napoleon no doubt made use of the offer, for in those early years books to him were as water to a parched throat, but Emilia, dark-haired, olive-skinned, also offered refreshment. As she walked with the General beneath the trees one warm summer evening the image of Désirée over in Marseille began to fade and he decided to marry Emilia. Hurrying into the house and finding the Countess alone he asked for the hand of her daughter. Mama fenced adroitly. She would have to ask her husband. The result was a refusal, not outright but sufficiently definite. 'You are in a position of responsibility and no doubt have a successful career before you. But remember you are a soldier and the country is at war. Who knows whether or not you will return with a whole skin from the Italian front? Again Emilia is very young. No, we must allow time to pass. If you are still of the same mind when hostilities have ceased ... well, time enough then to ask Emilia herself what she thinks about it.'

General Buonaparte retired in a huff. Opposition to his will, though not yet sacrilege, was irritating. When a few more years had passed nobody would dare question a decision of the Emperor, except such adroit rascals as Fouché or Talleyrand, who could conceal frowning dissent beneath smiling agreement. But here in the home of the Laurentis, aristocrats of the *Ancien Régime*, there stood only a young Corsican drawn from the superior peasantry, intelligent and ambitious, but of a social standing far below their own.

Had the Count or his wife known of the ardent letters their guest had written to Désirée Clary in Marseille only a week or two previously they would have listened to his request for the hand of their daughter with even less consideration. It was now early May. On 9 April he had written to Désirée, 'Yours to the end of time'. On 11 April, 'Your image is engraved on my heart. Never doubt of my love'. So few were her doubts that Désirée, had granted him the intimacy of her bedroom; a favour ill-repaid. Many years later the ex-Emperor was to say to Bertrand on Saint Helena, 'I made Bernadotte a marshal because I had taken Désirée's virginity'. An unworthy confession and in very bad taste.

The spring offensive of the Army of Italy had begun in the first week of April when Masséna, promoted a major-general after Toulon, crossed the frontier and entered Ventimiglia. Dumerbion had under his command some 43,000 hungry, ragged, unpaid, patriotic men, eager to fight, to die if need be, for a re-born France, for a future which was going to be quite different from the past, but which in so many ways would be just like the past; for revolutions do not change human nature.

The plan of operations called for a two-pronged attack. Masséna, advancing along the coast road as far as Oneglia, would afterwards swing left into the hills and capture Ormea. The first objective was to turn the left or eastern flank of the Piedmontese and separate them from their Austrian allies. Masséna's advance did not meet with serious opposition. Having seized Ormea he swung still further left and drove several thousand Piedmontese into the arms of Dumerbion advancing

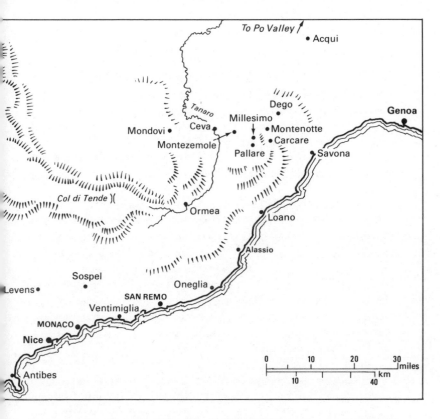

northward from Nice to Sospel and the Col di Tende. During these
operations Buonaparte, although given temporary command of three
infantry brigades in the advance on Oneglia and Ormea, played a
minor part. It was Masséna's day. Yet the plan had been drawn up by
'mon ami Buonaparte' at the request of Dumerbion, who, cautious to
the end, requested Commissioners Robespierre and Ricord to initial it
before saying the word go.

By the end of April the French held a line stretching from the Col di
Tende across the hills eastward and down to the sea at Loano. But this
was far from enough for the planner. Why stop half-way? The purpose
of war was not merely to inflict wounds on the enemy but to force him
to lay down his arms. Victory must be complete. This initial success
must be exploited, Piedmontese resistance crushed and King Amadeus

in Turin persuaded to sue for peace. At the very least the Army of Italy, destitute of supplies, should be encouraged to continue its advance down to the fertile plain of Mondovi across which flowed the Tanaro on its way to join the River Po, and where food would be available for the troops and fodder for the horses. If the Army of the Alps under General Kellermann could be encouraged to cooperate by making a simultaneous advance there would be no doubt as to the result. The lines of communication of both armies would be secure, the Austrians would be left as the sole enemy. The French would drive them back across Lombardy, right out of northern Italy, as Buonaparte had said.

Dumerbion, though restrained by caution, admired the clear and mature reasoning of his junior. The younger Robespierre and Citizen Ricord, it need hardly be said, agreed in advance. Augustin, who had recently reported on Buonaparte as 'an officer of exceptional merit', went himself to Paris to convince the Committee of Public Safety that the Army of Italy could bring about a decision with Austria. On arrival he found that Carnot, speaking for the committee, had other ideas: the Italian front was of secondary importance, the main effort would be launched across the Rhine into southern Germany. Nor must the Army of Italy forget that trouble could still arise in its rear, notably in Avignon and Toulon, where royalist sympathizers still lurked. However, Robespierre's brother could not be entirely rebuffed and Augustin returned with authority for a further limited advance into Piedmont; but it was given with reluctance and soon afterwards cancelled.

The summer passed with the French on the defensive and in the early autumn the Austrians decided to attack. This, however, merely gave Buonaparte the excuse for which he had been waiting and a report submitted by him to Paris tells the story of the Austrian failure.

The Austrians were threatening Savona and consequently the neutrality of Genoa. The Commissioners, convinced that there was no time to lose, ordered the Army of Italy to attack. We set off in September with a force composed of 12,000 infantry, 600 cavalry and some mountain artillery. On the morning 4 September [1794] we came in sight of the Austrians on the plain of Carcare. After we had occupied the heights in the vicinity of Pallare and Millesimo we decided to seize the old castle at that place and so threaten the rear of the enemy. As soon as Marshal Colardo became aware of the danger he began a retreat which was made in good order. The retreat continued throughout the night as far as Dego. At Carcare the inhabitants came out to us with the keys. We bivouacked on the field after getting our guns in position ready to bombard the enemy at first light. However, they decided not to await our attack but continued to retreat. The field of battle, all their stores at Dego together with their wounded fell into our hands. With three more hours of daylight this action at Dego would have cost the Emperor [of Austria] Lombardy.

So far so good. But Paris would allow no more and the campaign was to drag on for another eighteen months. Dumerbion was replaced by Kellermann, Kellermann by Schérer, the Army of Italy remaining on the defensive, the Austrians and the Piedmontese not wishing to risk another attack. In March 1796 Schérer was to hand over command to Buonaparte. The sword was at last drawn from the scabbard.

That success would have come about without a rehearsal of the first moves of the campaign cannot be doubted. The military genius of Buonaparte ensured success. In passing it can be recorded that no commander ever surpassed him at reading a map. He read it as a musician reads a score. As the latter, glancing at the printed notes, hears each played aloud, so did Buonaparte pouring over a map see, as though he were standing on the ground, every rise and fall, every twist and turn of a road or river, every obstacle which might facilitate or delay marching men. Even so it was certainly of great advantage to him to launch his first campaign over land he had previously ridden and fought across. From the crest of Montezemole he had surveyed the approach to Turin, and had looked across the valley of the Tanaro to the distant Alps. Walking his horse back down the road from Carcare to Savona he had registered every turn, noting in particular that the surface was fit for the passage of guns and supply wagons; for it was up this same road that he would order his main column to advance eighteen months later when he was in supreme command.

Meanwhile back at army headquarters in Nice he turned to his duties as Commander of Coast Defences. Pursuing the habit he had formed at Toulon he bombarded the War Ministry with a ceaseless stream of letters, reports, requests and observations, most of them dictated to the faithful Junot.

On 16 June, that is to say during the interval between the first and second phase of that modest advance into Italy, a strongly worded protest against interference by the navy was in the despatch case of a courier galloping across France on his way to Paris where Citizen Pillé of the Committee for the Army and Navy duly found waiting on his desk the following terse, unambiguous letter.

I enclose a map of Gulf Juan which please bring to the notice of the Committee of Public Safety. Send four 12 inch mortars for the Gulf. They are essential.

I must inform you that Admiral Thévenard at Port-La-Montagne (Toulon) is interfering with my orders to the detriment of the service. He is hoarding too many guns there at the expense of other parts of the coast. Kindly make clear to the Admiral that all matters relating to artillery are the business of gunners. It is I who am responsible for the defence of the coast from Marseille to Menton, apart from my position as commander of the artillery of the Army of Italy. Nothing but confusion arises when officers exceed their appointed functions.

Having put Admiral Thévenard in his place Buonaparte gave his attention to the conduct of more junior officers under his direct command, among them a certain Berlier in charge of the Antibes district.

I am most dissatisfied with the lack of progress at La Brague. There is neither powder, shot, nor gunners. All should have been completed within twenty-four hours. Corporal Carli is to be placed under arrest for absenting himself from duty in order to fetch wine from Antibes. Instruct all battery commanders that in no circumstances is any man to leave his post. Inform me as soon as the 24-pounders have arrived.

Chapter 11

The end of Terror

On the morning of 27 July 1794, known at the time as the 9th Thermidor, Maximilien Robespierre walked the short distance from 366 rue Saint Honoré to the House of Representatives in the Tuileries Palace nearby. Except for the orangery, which now houses priceless Impressionist paintings, the palace has disappeared, burnt down during another revolution. The Hotel Maurice stands on the site of the riding school where the representatives of the people, known as the National Convention, discussed the future of France.

Maurice Duplay, a cabinet maker who owned 366 rue Saint Honoré and lived there with his wife, his son and his three sisters, had offered a room to Robespierre some three years before. A kind man, he respected Maximilien as a man of honour in pursuit of an ideal, as the saviour of a troubled France seeking its way towards a better future. Madame Duplay, nearer to earth, saw in him the perfect lodger, unmarried, reserved, modest, abstemious, virtuous, tidy in his room, immaculate in dress. On this particular July day he was wearing the sky-blue coat with broad lapels he had had made for the Feast of the Supreme Being a few weeks previously, a lace cravat, white knee breeches and stockings. His hair was carefully combed and powdered. There had never been anything of the unwashed, *sans-culotte* mob leader about this young lawyer from Arras.

The admiration which Duplay and his wife felt for Maximilien was shared by Eléonore, one of Maurice's three sisters, to whose admiration was added unchanging love. Another sister, Elizabeth, had married Citizen Lebas, Maximilien's loyal friend. Eléonore's love, alas, met only friendship. Her relationship with the dictator knew no greater intimacy than an evening walk with the dog. On this July day the two friends could not know that yesterday's walk had been their last, that within a few hours Eléonore would be left to lament the death of her beloved. And with her love ran deep, for she mourned him through fifty long years to the hour of her own death.

The road that had led Robespierre to power was short, some five years; to supreme power much shorter, a few months only. But today he was master of France, unchallenged, feared by all. In youth he had been sent by his parents to be educated in Paris at the college of Louis-le-Grand, after which he returned to his native Arras to practise law. But fate had other work for him. It began on 5 April 1789 when the States General, summoned by Louis XVI, met at Versailles. Robespierre, then aged thirty-one, was elected to represent the Arras region as a member of the Third Estate which might be compared to the professional class of today, though at the time it was small fry. One hundred and seventy-five years had passed since the Estates had met. It was part of history. Louis XIII was then on the throne of France, the Sun King had still to challenge his subjects with 'L'Etat c'est Moi'. In those days the Third Estate considered it a privilege to sit in the same chamber with their betters, the nobility and the clergy, to whom they doffed their hats, bowing low. But today all would be different. The Third Estate had come of age. Its members were no longer poor relations, flattered to be seated at the table of the rich. They had become conscious of representing a growing, more prosperous, better educated class of citizen. They would not forget their manners; but tradition must not be allowed to fetter them nor fear to bar the path of duty.

The decision to summon the States General was a gesture of despair. France, though nobody would admit the fact, was bankrupt. The States General could no more hold off disaster than could the French Government of 1940, when, led by Monsieur Deladier, its members knelt in Notre Dame praying for salvation while German tanks raced towards Paris.

In recent years the ship of state had been kept afloat by the tireless pumping of the Swiss banker, Necker, surely the world's champion borrower – unless we look around us in England today. But the day of reckoning had come, as it inevitably must, whether to the individual or to the group of individuals known as the State. The creditors of France were no longer willing to accept such collateral as she could offer. They had had enough. Necker therefore vanished from the scene and was replaced by Monsieur Callone who in turn made room for Cardinal Lomenie de Brienne, an aristocrat of the Church who had no apparent difficulty in reconciling rank and wealth with the teaching of Jesus.

Each of these having nothing better to offer than increased taxation – more especially a tax on land which would hit the nobility and the clergy – followed Necker into the wings, speeded on their way by cries of indignation from all who had great possessions. Again Necker was summoned to the rescue. But his day was done. He could only repeat his well-known borrowing act, now more sterile than ever. He was not only dismissed but banished to his native Switzerland.

During all this the King, behind his protective wall of the ritual of Versailles, remained silent, though it may be presumed that when the suggestion to summon the States General reached him he shrugged his fat shoulders despairingly. His divinity-hedged great-great-grand-father, Louis XIV, might have solved the financial problem which he and his wars had created. But who could expect kind, stupid, vacillating, unfortunate Louis XVI to ask, 'Will this help? Whither does it lead?' It led to the French Revolution.

There were, of course, other contributions. Men had begun increasingly to think, to ask themselves, and others when they dared, such questions as, 'Is the King really divine or only partly? And if partly which part?'

Maximilien Robespierre was among the questioners. He had come a long way since he had stood in the Tennis Court at Versailles and, a very junior member of the Third Estate, had, when his turn came to stand before President Bailly, sworn that famous oath that no power on earth should dissolve its members until their work was done. A few weeks later he had heard the name of the Third Estate changed to the National Assembly, had seen even members of the nobility and the clergy join its rebellious ranks. Despotism was of the past; liberty and equality should now reign in its place; happiness was at hand for the people of France. Neither he nor any of the enthusiastic men beside him sensed anything more than a change for the better. They could not foresee that revolution would become a tidal wave destroying all in its path, including themselves. 'Watch lest there should arise in France a citizen so redoubtable that one day he becomes the master.' When later, in one of his well-prepared speeches, Robespierre gave this warning he can hardly have meant that citizen to be himself, though for a short period the two were one.

By pursuing an unswerving course, by taking virtue as his guide and refusing all compromise, Robespierre had reached the summit of power. He had become 'the Incorruptible'. He was so incorruptible that he could see his friends, including those who had helped him to power, put to death rather than that they should persist in error, or what had appeared to him to be error. Yet his early training never deserted him. All must be done within the law. If no law existed permitting the necessary conviction and punishment then the freely elected Representatives of the People must be persuaded to enact one. And which Representative would dare to oppose what was so clearly for the universal good? Only a traitor. By June 1794, when the Law of Prairial was passed, allowing no counsel for the defence of those brought before the Revolutionary Tribunal and no verdict other than acquittal or death, Robespierre had become the Holy Inquisitor who, prayer-book in one hand, red-hot poker in the other, stood ready to encourage the weak or persuade the sinful to read aloud the sacred words. He had become a dangerous man. But on this morning July 1794 he himself was walking towards danger.

Nearing the riding school his mind perhaps went back to the Feast of the Supreme Being which had taken place on a sunny morning a few weeks ago. The idea had been his own. A country could not be governed without a religious background, but the old God served by a priesthood deriving its power from superstition must go. The new God should be the God of Reason, the Supreme Being. The pageant had been admirably staged by Jacques Louis David, the official artist. It included such effects as young bulls drawing chariots, young girls showering flowers and a specially constructed hill crowned by a Tree of Liberty. Boys came forward to hand their fathers muskets with which to defend *La Patrie*. In all it was a fine show and the weather was ideal. But, leading the procession, inclining his plumed head right and left in reply to cries of '*Vive Robespierre*', he had overheard jealous whisperings from behind: 'Does he think he is God?'

Yet if Fouché and other evil minds were working for his downfall, well, that was the fate of all just men. He, the upholder of virtue whose life was an open book, need have no fear. Intrigue would recoil upon itself. Friends were at hand; the loyalty of Saint Just, of Couthon and others need never be doubted. And behind them were the people of France. Like Caesar, he might disregard the Ides of March; he approached the Capitol fearless, convinced that no man would dare to strike him down. But, like Caesar, he was to fall.

The day before, addressing the Convention, he had given warning of the treachery which remained to be crushed, had uttered ominous threats, had foretold the fate of all enemies of the people, but had mentioned none by name. Saint Just would read out the list tomorrow. It was a fatal mistake, for when Robespierre had finished speaking each man was left with the question, 'Is it I?' It gave time for Fouché and other artful men to hurry from one member of the Convention to another whispering, 'Your name is on the list. Strike before it is too late.' The courage of despair blossomed and when Robespierre entered the chamber and Saint Just mounted the tribune, list in hand, angry voices were raised against both, 'Down with the tyrant'. Robespierre, attempting to intervene, could not be heard against the chorus of hate. Collot d'Herbois, chairman of the day, was on the side of the conspirators. Cassius and Casca, assuming the shapes of Barras, of Tallien, or Fréron, plunged no daggers into Robespierre but their vengeance was as swift and as cruel. Within twenty-four hours, reviled by the mob which had so recently cheered him with wild applause, Maximilien Robespierre was hurried to the guillotine to which he had sent so many others. With him perished his brother Augustin, Saint Just, Couthon, twenty in all. On the following day so fiercely did the fire of vengeance burn that to these twenty were added another seventy-one. Robespierre and his party had disappeared into a bloody basket. The terror he had intended should now end had ended him.

On the eve of Robespierre's death Brigadier-General Buonaparte, returning from Genoa, landed at Nice. He had been sent to Genoa by Commissioner Ricord to see the French Ambassador to that neutral state and to ascertain how far its neutrality could be counted on during continued hostilities against Austria and Piedmont. His mission accomplished, he returned to report to Army Headquarters and resume his duty as commander of the artillery. He lodged as usual at the home of the Laurentis in the rue Villefranche. Count Laurenti and his wife were there to welcome him, though they had prudently sent Emilia to stay at the family's country home near Grasse. The three dining together could not guess at the tragedy which had taken place in Paris, nor was the news of the fall of Robespierre widely known in the south until 5 August. To the Laurentis and their friends it could only bring relief. To others, especially to any active in politics, it was a danger signal. Such men as Carnot, creator of France's seven revolutionary armies, might hold their own, as could Barras, Fréron and others. But in general to all connected, however remotely, with the previous government it was instantly important to prove that one had never been a follower of the fallen giant, better still that one had been on the point of rebelling against him. Cautious natures like that of General Dumerbion could still retire to bed with the fair assurance of not being awakened at four in the morning by anything more unpleasant than a twinge of gout. Others, Commissioners attached to an army, members of the National Convention, men like Saliceti, Gaspari or Ricord, had to be wary. Even Commissioner Turreau's honeymoon must have been disturbed by the thought of danger. Was he sure that his influential friends in Paris would stand by him in case of trouble? Indeed, were they still alive?

In the case of General Buonaparte the avengers of terror need not hesitate. He was an obvious victim, an intimate friend of Robespierre's brother, on good terms with their sister Charlotte (to his credit, when in power he granted her a life pension), a known Jacobin sympathizer. What an excellent target for those who were anxious to direct attention away from themselves. Yet one would hardly have expected fellow-Corsican Saliceti to be the one to aim the first blow. However, Saliceti had recently been transferred from the Army of Italy to the Army of the Alps where feelings, ruled by jealousy, were far from friendly. Why, it was asked, should the former have been given preference by Paris in the matter of supplies? It could only be favouritism due to the influence of the younger Robespierre. Whatever the reason, on 6 August, a few hours after learning of the fall of both brothers, Saliceti wrote to a friend:

> I have just heard that the tyrant and his friends have been executed. I am filled with joy. You remember how the Army of Italy was

completely in the hands of Augustin and Ricord. I am sure that as soon as I reach Nice Ricord will have fled, also no doubt Buonaparte. If they are still there we have decided to place them under arrest and send them to Paris.

Worse was to follow. A week later General Buonaparte wrote to Monsieur Tilly, French Ambassador in Genoa:

You will have heard of the conspiracy of Robespierre, Saint Just and Couthon. I was rather pained by the fate of Augustin whom I liked and believed to be honest, but had he been my own father, if he aspired to tyranny I would have stabbed him to the heart.

There is an expression known to actors as 'ham' which fits this outburst of Corsican emotion, this sound and fury signifying not very much, except perhaps a moment of panic. Nor is the condemnation of tyranny by one on his way to becoming a tyrant without irony.

Chapter 12

General Buonaparte under arrest

> General Buonaparte commanding the Artillery of the Army of Italy is hereby suspended from duty. He is to be placed in arrest and sent to Paris under escort.

This unpleasant communication, signed by Saliceti, was delivered to army headquarters in Nice early in August, 1794. If, as is probable, it was read out by Dumerbion to Buonaparte standing before his desk it is not difficult to imagine the embarrassment of the army Commander nor the incredible surprise of Buonaparte. So this was what Saliceti called friendship!

Having issued the order on his own initiative and feeling perhaps that it needed emphasis, Saliceti followed it by a report to the Ministry of War:

> General Buonaparte, having forfeited the confidence of the Representatives of the People by his suspicious conduct, more especially by his recent journey to Genoa, the Representatives have decided to send him to Paris under escort.

This was signed by Commissioners Saliceti, Albitte and Laporte, determined to prove their loyalty to the victors of today by handing over to them one of the losers of yesterday. Yet one would have thought that Saliceti, if he really meant business, could have done better. Of what did 'suspicious conduct' consist? And he and his friends had pitted themselves against a fellow commissioner exercising powers equal to theirs, for Buonaparte had been sent to Genoa by order of Commissioner Ricord. Or was it that being a politician Saliceti wished to avoid a situation from which he could not retreat at the appropriate moment? Who knew which party might seize power tomorrow?

The old, experienced fox, when the hounds draw too near, crosses his scent with that of a younger, more vigorous fox; but once the hounds have been called off and the danger to both has passed, he bears his saviour no ill will. Fear prompted his artful, unfriendly act; fear guided the treacherous hand of Saliceti, and fear being removed, friendship, such as it was, returned. General Buonaparte's arrest had no unpleasant consequences. The hounds being thrown off the scent, the commissioners could afford generosity, their victim could breathe more freely.

> Having examined his papers and correspondence we are of the opinion that nothing of a positive nature warrants the continued detention of this officer.

Buonaparte was imprisoned locally in Fort Carré, Antibes, from where, after an unpleasant two weeks, he was released and no more was heard of his being sent to Paris. He was free to rejoin his family at Château Sallé and to resume his duties with the army. Meanwhile his two weeks detention had been put to good use – he had filled the hours of enforced leisure by studying Marshal Maillebois' Piedmont campaign of 1745.

It has been claimed by a popular French historian, André Castelot, that Buonaparte, while under arrest, was allowed to remain in the Laurenti home in Nice, Count Laurenti standing guarantee for him and a sentry on duty before the door; that the long-believed story of his detention in Fort Carré at Antibes is only legend. This can hardly be correct. Buonaparte may well have been allowed to remain overnight with his host, but he was certainly transferred without delay to the greater security of the fort where he not only studied an earlier campaign in northern Italy, but pleaded his innocence to the Committee of Public Safety and wrote numerous other letters, among them one dated 12 August to this faithful Aide-de-Camp, Junot, who was planning his escape. In general terms the letter read:

To Lieutenant Junot   Antibes
Aide-de-Camp to General Buonaparte   12 August 1794

What you suggest, my dear Junot, clearly proves your friendship for me. You have long known mine for you and that you can depend on it. Men may be unjust to me, my dear Junot, but it is enough that I am innocent. My conscience is the tribunal before which I stand. When I examine my conscience I find it clear. So do nothing. You will only compromise me.

> Au revoir, dear Junot
> Buonaparte (under arrest)

A more dignified letter than the one he had written a few days previously to the French Ambassador in Genoa.

It was fortunate that the proposed journey to Paris under escort did not take place. In the atmosphere of unreasoned hatred, suspicion and revenge which reigned, in which heads were falling like autumn leaves, what chance would a junior brigadier-general owing his promotion to the favouritism of the fallen tyrant have had before the Revolutionary Tribunal? Moreover the People's Representatives on the spot would never have wasted public money sending him to Paris under escort unless they were convinced of his guilt. Their authority must be upheld, their zeal encouraged. There were generals in plenty – Jourdan, Hoche, Kellermann – men of talent and considerably more experience.

After a joyous reunion with his family, Buonaparte returned to army headquarters in Nice where he was warmly welcomed by Dumerbion who had stood by him loyally, even braving the wrath of the Commissioners by praising him after his arrest. 'Officers of his ability are rare,' he had written to Carnot. And again at the conclusion of the autumn campaign occasioned by the sudden, but badly led Austrian counter-offensive which resulted in their being driven back to Acqui well beyond the starting point, his words were equally generous. 'Our success has been due to the intelligent suggestions of the commander of the Artillery.' Dumerbion was a gentleman.

After her son's release from prison Madame Mère, perhaps finding the atmosphere of Antibes uncongenial, removed to Marseille, taking with her her three daughters and Louis and Jerome. Before they left, however, Joseph and his plain, dull, rich wife whom he had married on 1 August at Cuges, near Marseille, came to spend a short honeymoon at Antibes. Julie's sister, Désirée, accompanied them, renewing the flames in Buonaparte's fickle heart. But the happy interlude was not to last. Joseph and Julie were on their way to Genoa, Buonaparte and Junot about to resume military duty, the others already preparing for the journey to Marseille.

Today Château Sallé stands a decaying relic of eighteenth-century elegance; crumbling stonework falls from its twin towers, its windows are clouded with dust, or cracked. Below, through what was then the garden, still runs the stream in which the Buonaparte girls rinsed the household linen, though it is hard to find, being narrowly enclosed by concrete walls, and afterwards disappearing beneath a block of unsightly flats. The château itself has been split into lodgings for municipal workers and washing hangs from the balcony.

Autumn drew on. In Paris revenge reigned and terror continued to hunt down terror. Citizen Carrier, who had fraternally sunk bargeloads of priests and nuns and other enemies of the people beneath the waters of the Loire, received his reward from the Republic One and Indivisible, though hardly in the shape he anticipated. That his accusers described him as a cannibal must have seemed to him ungrateful, though it does bring truth to the saying that revolutions devour their young. Another who fell was the Public Prosecutor himself, Fouquier-Tinville. Denounced by Citizen Fréron, the suitor of Pauline Buonaparte, it did not avail Fouquier to plead 'I only obeyed orders'. Though he was to linger a further six months in gaol, he joined the many he had sent to their death early in 1795.

While vengeance pursued its way in Paris, in the south the campaign paused for breath. The Army of Italy having received orders to remain entirely on the defensive in Piedmont, its artillery commander was freed for other duties, and these took him again to Toulon, still called Port-of-the-Mountain. In December he said goodbye to Count and Countess Laurenti and moved to Marseille where his mother and the rest of the family now lived.

The duties he was assigned included the preparation of an expeditionary force destined for the liberation of Corsica. But had not Corsica been an integral part of France for the past twenty-five years? The confusion arises form the different meaning given to words by different men. Those who die for an idea are hailed by some as heroes, by others reviled as traitors.

Time from its lofty seat of judgement assesses the rival claims and awards the prize. Though the contestants are no longer present to receive their reward all is not lost, for their descendants may learn from it toleration and reason. Thus to Corsicans and their beloved Paoli liberty meant one thing, to France, revolutionary or royalist, another. It is a common saying in France even today that the world is divided into five continents – and Corsica. Two hundred years ago the situation was different: laws, decrees, threats and retribution cried aloud in Paris left those who voted for or voiced them frustrated, whilst Corsicans remained unmoved.

Some Corsicans, such as the Pozzo di Borgo family, clung to Paoli, others, including the Buonapartes and their friend Saliceti, remained loyal to France. 'I was fond of Paoli, but he espoused the cause of England, I, that of France. Paoli used to pat me on the head when I was a young man, saying: "You are one of Plutarch's men".' This was said by Emperor Napoleon when a prisoner on Saint Helena, recalling the days when he was a precocious fifteen and Paoli a man of forty.

Saliceti was to share with General Buonaparte in the organization of the expeditionary force destined to drive the English from Corsica. For it was they who, at the invitation of Paoli, had seized the island. But before coming to that, it is necessary to turn back and trace the events which led Napoleon to say twenty years later, 'Paoli went over to the English. I remained loyal to France'.

Chapter 13

Corsica breaks its bonds

Pasquale Paoli, after his flight from Corsica on board an English ship in 1769, lived in England for the next twenty-one years. He had welcomed the severance of his homeland from an indifferent, bankrupt Genoa, but deplored its transference to an aggressive France, determined that in future there should be no mistake as to who was master. Paoli's long exile in England was, however, not unpleasant, nor without compensation. He came as a welcome guest. It was not long since the publication of Boswell's *Journal of a Tour to Corsica*, in which he had praised Paoli as the ideal ruler, the champion of every just man. George III received him at Windsor, the Government voted him an allowance of £1,200 a year, and every door of eighteenth-century London was open to him. John Wesley, to his regret, just missed greeting him on his arrival at Portsmouth, Boswell hurried to call on him in Bond Street where he first lodged. Samuel Johnson, Reynolds, Garrick and Horace Walpole were among his friends. The allowance paid him by the Treasury enabled him not only to live in comfort but to help many of those friends who had fled with him rather than accept life in French-occupied Corsica.

Paoli liked and admired his English hosts, though not blindly: 'Whenever they confer a favour they always calculate the profit they may derive from it.' Only prejudice or ignorance can refute this variation of Napoleon's 'The English are a nation of shopkeepers', though Paoli can hardly have been referring to his own case, for the

71

English were unlikely to derive much profit from an annual gift of £1,200 multiplied by an unforeseeable number of years. He was in fact destined to reside in England during thirty-four of his eighty-two years, all at the expense of the British people.

When revolution broke out in France in 1789 it brought with it the opportunity for Paoli to return to his homeland. Right of birth, privilege based on descent from a noble line, or ascent upon the ecclesiastical ladder, were swept away. Opportunity shone a new light on every man's path. In French eyes it followed that Paoli, the apostle of freedom, must return to Corsica, recently created one of the eighty-three departments of a new France. The tyranny of kings was over. A new era had dawned over a new Corsica. Who better than a true Corsican, one who had endured exile for love of his country, to lead it on its new road along which it would share the destiny of a powerful, more friendly France?

One year after the outbreak of the Revolution an optimistic French Government invited Paoli to return to Corsica. Travelling via Paris he was given an ovation at the Bar of the National Assembly and met on that occasion a young fellow Corsican, Christofano Saliceti. He was received in audience by King Louis XVI, whom he found to be 'charming and gracious', and invited to stand beside Lafayette at a revue of the National Guard. Paoli had become a national figure.

Continuing his journey down the valley of the Rhone he was cheered and fêted at every shop. At Aix-en-Provence he was met by Joseph Buonaparte, son of his friend Charles of former days, also by Pozzo di Borgo who was to be a staunch friend in the future. Both accompanied him during the remainder of his journey, though the feelings of the two last towards one another could scarcely have been warm. The di Borgo family had occupied the floor above the Buonapartes in the rue Malherbe in Ajaccio. The two families had never been on cordial terms and feelings were not improved when Signora di Borgo had emptied a chamber-pot on to the head of one of the Buonapartes below. It was all a long time ago and the incident trivial, but the two families never drew close. Political ideals held them apart, and the rift widened with time and the rise to power of Napoleon.

When Paoli finally set foot on Corsican soil on 17 July 1790 – a year and three days after the fall of the Bastille – he was deeply moved. Twenty-one years, during which hope must often have been overshadowed by despair, had been a long time of waiting. But now his reward had come. Paoli was received by cheering crowds. He was Corsica's hero who, having suffered for his people, now returned triumphant.

In France that summer the Revolution was in its heyday, still, as it were, enjoying a year-long honeymoon. None could foresee, or, foreseeing, avert the tragedy ahead. Before another year had passed revolution, gathering speed, would begin an uncontrolled rush, all brakes failing; within another three it would take France by the throat and strangle liberty in the name of liberty. But now the sun shone, the year's harvest promised to be good, France was at peace with her neighbours, all was glorious within and without. What could be more desirable to the island lovers of liberty than to share in the happy scene? *Liberté, Egalité, Fratérnité* echoed from across the sea like distant church bells announcing the arrival on earth of men of goodwill.

It was too good to last. Tyranny has never been the monopoly of kings. Misunderstandings, glossed over in the beginning, refused to be ignored. As the months went by it became ever clearer that liberty and equality had one meaning to Frenchmen on the mainland and another to the inhabitants of Corsica. Freedom, liberty, equality and the rest, all that was splendid, provided tradition, ancient customs and sacred beliefs, were respected. And among the sacred beliefs was vendetta. Family feuds lasting through generations must come first, grandsons must be allowed to avenge insults to grandfathers in the name of honour, men to murder each other in the same cause and afterwards escape to the maquis, where again honour forbade the rare inhabitants to disclose the fugitive's hiding place to the police. Even Paoli, who never shared in this elementary creed, could do little to discourage it.

More than sentiment or attachment to crude forms of justice separated Corsicans from Frenchmen. The desire for independence which had driven Paoli and others into exile still existed. But independence had its price. Corsica could not stand alone in a fast-developing world. Lieutenant Buonaparte, returning on leave from his first garrison in Valence, had recognized the fact. Fiercely Corsican, bitterly anti-French as he had been at school in Brienne, or even at Valence, his superior intelligence had overcome prejudice. He sensed that the island's economy could only survive if fused with that of a powerful neighbour, and since, shortly before his birth, Corsica had become a French possession, the way to the future was clear.

By returning to Corsica at the invitation of the French Government it might appear that Paoli, too, had accepted union with France. But his acceptance was outward and conditional. Italy – more precisely Genoa – was in the past and could be forgotten. France was here and now and had greeted him as a national hero. Nevertheless Corsica was not the Isle of Wight. The rift widened with the years. Revolution cast a lurid, deepening shadow. The execution of the King extinguished the last ray of hope.

Paoli turned again to England. He had long experience of slow English thought, of England's more gradual progress towards the idea of liberty, towards the abolition of privilege. True, the English, too, had murdered their king, but that was a hundred and fifty years ago. There had been time for them to come to their senses, to recognize that violence only led to more violence, that law and order alone made for the happiness of the people. Rule by Parliament, despite hollow words and argument leading nowhere, false promises, hypocrisy, the guile of men seeking only self-advancement, despite the slow, creaking machinery of government, did in the end triumph over bloody revolution.

All that had begun so well in 1790 had turned sour during the ensuing three years. Paoli, with ninety per cent of Corsica behind him, had had enough. In June, 1793, an Anglo-Spanish fleet cruised off the coast of Corsica without arousing hostile feelings among the inhabitants, who, from the shore, could see the colour of the flags, and in August of that year Lord Grenville, Foreign Secretary under Pitt, received a letter from Paoli asking upon what terms England would be willing to assume responsibility for Corsica's political existence? While this request was no doubt greeted in Downing Street with satisfied, even jubilant, sidelong glances and a metaphorical rubbing of hands (how splendidly the investment of £1,200 a year over twenty years had paid off!) the Committee of Public Safety in Paris received the news with less enthusiasm. Paoli, Pozzo di Borgo and twenty-five of their followers were proclaimed traitors and outlawed. Since France had been at war with England during the previous five months this was a normal reaction, though its result was merely to drive Corsica further into the arms of the enemy. Agreement with England was not reached without the usual Corsican reservations, but for the moment these were silenced by the urgent need for foreign help by one party, and by the other the fact that Corsican harbours would now be reserved for British warships sailing in the Mediterranean.

In due course an English delegation headed by Sir Gilbert Elliot arrived in Corsica. Lieutenant-Colonel John Moore was in command and had under him a junior officer named Hudson Lowe. The former was to find death and fame at Corunna; the latter became, some twenty years later, the frightened, narrow-minded, petty gaoler of General Buonaparte on a lonely island in the southern Atlantic.

Some parts of Corsica were at the time still garrisoned by French troops and here resistance was encountered. There was fighting, mainly conducted by the Navy, at Bastia, and in the summer of 1794 Captain Nelson, holding the temporary rank of Colonel of Marines, lost the sight of one eye at Calvi. 'I got a little hurt this morning', he said. Later in the summer, one week after the death of Robespierre, when less honest and possibly less violent men had risen to power, Corsica formally acknowledged the King of England, George III, as the island's rightful monarch, though on what grounds it would be hard to say. Sir Gilbert Elliot was elevated to Viceroy and was later joined by charming, sociable Lady Elliot and many friends. Hostilities ceased and were replaced by gay parties. Corsica took on the appearance of an English colony.

France, furious and vengeful, sought to drive out the foreigner and recover the sovereignty rightly hers. Corsica must be liberated. Perfidious Albion must be taught a lesson.

The Expeditionary Force gathering at Toulon, under the direction of Commissioner Saliceti and seconded by General Buonaparte, was chosen as the means of liberation. But things moved slowly and it was March 1795 before the expedition set sail: and when it did it failed as miserably as General Buonaparte had foretold. From the day he had received orders to serve with it he had known and had said openly that so long as English warships controlled the Mediterranean Corsica would remain out of reach.

On 14 March 1795 fifteen French ships of war were met at sea by fourteen English ships under the command of Admiral Hotham. The action was brief, the only active part being played by Captain Nelson in the *Agamemnon*. The French made a run for it and most of their ships reached the shelter of Toulon harbour, humbled but afloat. Two of their number, the *Ça-Ira* and the *Censeur*, were captured and towed into San Firenzo at the northern end of Corsica. The island they had set out to liberate received them as prisoners.

If General Buonaparte did not say aloud, 'I told you so', he was certainly entitled to do so. But as usual the Ministry of War had the last word, for, as we shall see, he was reduced in rank shortly afterwards and transferred to another theatre of operations.

In the end the English themselves liberated Corsica, peacefully and without bloodshed – an unexpected solution, for England had, until recently, the reputation of being a guest who overstayed her welcome. The departure of the English from Corsica may have been hastened by the rapid conquest of northern Italy in 1796 by a French army under General Bonaparte (he dropped the Italian-sounding 'u' upon assuming command). Whatever the reason, Sir Gilbert Elliot and his small court were recalled and the last of the occupying force sailed from Corsica on 12 October of that year. The French then resumed possession and Corsica has remained a part of France ever since.

One year before the English occupying forces withdrew, Pascale Paoli returned to England at the invitation of George III. Paoli was then sixty-eight and suffering from arthritis, though this painful disease was not to prevent him living to the age of eighty-two. He died in 1807 and was buried at his own request without ceremony in the churchyard of Saint Pancras, reserved at the time as a resting place for members of the Roman Catholic religion. His grave bore the inscription 'Pascal Paoli. Once supreme head and legislator of Corsica'. England recognized his worth by erecting a memorial in Westminster Abbey below which amid lengthy words of praise may be read: 'One of the most eminent and most illustrious characters of the age in which he lived. He was elected unanimously supreme leader of Corsica at the age of thirty-three'.

In the year 1889, by which time France was enjoying her third republic, Paoli's body was taken back to Corsica at Corsican expense by the British Navy and re-interred in his native village, Morosaglia. Although eight years had passed since his death the love of the Corsicans for a leader of integrity devoid of self-interest lived on. Every commune on the island – and some were very poor – contributed willingly and proudly to the expense involved in his homecoming. No man could wish for greater praise.

Chapter 14

Towards Paris

After the futility of trying to liberate Corsica had been accepted by Carnot and his regional representative, Saliceti, General Buonaparte found himself stationed in Toulon without much to do. Those few weeks between March and April 1795 were, until his downfall, the most leisurely he was ever to know. He was no longer attached to the Army of Italy, where Dumerbion had been replaced by Kellermann, and the coastal defences which had kept him busy during the previous year were now in good shape and needed only occasional inspection.

Since the fall of Robespierre the political pendulum had swung from what today would be called the extreme left. Although Napoleon had so far been the only member of the family to be imprisoned, and then only for two weeks, Joseph, Lucien and Uncle Fesch had all lost their jobs. To Joseph this was not of importance. He was financially independent and he and Julie were often in Genoa where the Clarys had business connections. Uncle Fesch and Lucien were not so fortunate. The former made his way to Paris where, as a member of the priesthood, he might find employment; the latter, plain Lucien Buonaparte now, leaving his wife and their baby daughter, Christine Charlotte, in Saint Maximin, disappeared in the region of Sète, a minor Mediterranean port, where for a time he found humble employment and a hiding place from the many he had denounced as enemies of the people and who were now out for his blood. The rest of the family were in Marseille, where Letitzia did her best to make ends meet with

77

an allowance from the state and such money as her son could spare from his pay.

Not busily employed at the time, General Buonaparte found time to visit Marseille. He was a frequent guest in the Clary home where Désirée Clary was a potent attraction. Rapidly fading into the past now were the evening walks with Emilia Laurenti beneath the orchard trees of the rue Villefranche in Nice and the inviting glances of Citizeness Turreau.

The immediate foreground was now filled by Désirée. With youthful ardour Napoleon spoke of marriage, though without, it seems, asking her parents for her hand, as was the custom. Had he done so his request might well have been answered as before: 'One Buonaparte is enough', for although his mother would have welcomed a further union with the wealthy Clary family, Madame Clary was less enthusiastic.

Meanwhile, during the first days of May, the happy hours were suddenly interrupted by orders from the War Ministry instructing General Buonaparte to report for duty in the Vendée where the Army of the West was engaged in repulsing attacks by royalist rebels encouraged and supported by the British. Far more unpleasant than this transfer to the relatively quiet west when France was actively engaged with professional armies on her eastern frontier, and where promotion was possible, was the fact that he was appointed to the command of an infantry brigade. The administrative branch of the Ministry, perhaps stirred by the failure of the Corsican venture, had decided that there were far too many officers of general rank in the south, especially in the artillery. The most junior (Buonaparte was no. 139) must either be placed on the unemployed list or transferred to another arm. General Buonaparte did not agree. Discipline was all right for others, but not for him. An infantry brigade when his whole training, indeed his whole heart, was with the guns? No, his future was with the artillery or nowhere. In any case there could be little hope of advancement with the Army of the West engaged in civil war. True, he had fought against his own countrymen at Toulon. But he was a junior major then with a reputation to make. There had been no other choice. Yet what choice was there now? Resignation? That would be dangerous. It might be accepted. (That polite form of blackmail he was to hold in reserve for a later date when success made the risk worthwhile.) Wisely he fell back on the well-worn method of applying for sick-leave. It would at least gain time and provide an opportunity to visit Paris and plead his case with the authorities.

When, on 8 May, Buonaparte, with a total disregard of orders, set off for Paris he was accompanied by a small court of his own choosing, namely Junot, Marmont and his brother Louis, aged sixteen. The first two had now attained the rank of Captain; Louis, without training or experience, had been granted a commission through the influence of citizen Turreau. He was to remain only a month with his brother in Paris before being admitted as a cadet to the School of Artillery at Châlons, from where in the following autumn he was gazetted into the 4th Artillery, Napoleon's original regiment. Throughout his life Napoleon acted as a kind father to Louis, though the latter did not invariably show gratitude.

Captain Junot accompanied Napoleon as his Aide-de-Camp, Marmont, it would seem, out of personal loyalty, which, lasting through twenty years, was to be wrongfully questioned when his Emperor had lost all sense of proportion, when victorious enemies stood at the gates of Paris and the only hope of saving the remnants of Empire lay in surrender.

Arriving at Avignon, the four were entertained at dinner by the local commander whose Aide-de-Camp was a young cavalry officer, not very clever nor much of a soldier, but of good family, attractive in appearance and a darling of the ladies. The officer's name was Hippolyte Charles. Had General Buonaparte been able to see a short way into the future, their meeting would not have been cordial, for Hippolyte was soon to console in amorous embrace Josephine de Beauharnais not long after she became Madame Buonaparte.

Nearing Paris, Buonaparte and his small court were the guests of Monsieur and Madame Marmont at Châtillon-sur-Seine. Overjoyed to see their son who had been on active service both at Toulon and in Italy, they would no doubt have preferred to hear about his personal adventures rather than be forced to listen to an interminable discourse on the political and military situation of France from his friend. But in future years when her son became Duc de Raguse and a Marshal of France and his friend an Emperor, Madame Marmont perhaps recalled that evening with mixed feelings of amusement and pride. Meanwhile her husband, bidding goodbye to their guests next day, gave some advice to the General whose advanced ideas had perhaps given him cause to think before going to sleep. 'Do not rush things. Allow time for this revolution to settle down. The propertied class may still come into its own, and may need you.' This was wise counsel, although riches and power would largely be in other hands by the time the ambitious General assumed control.

Before reaching Paris Napoleon found what he knew to be an excellent opportunity of helping his brother Joseph: 'Yesterday I visited an estate belonging to Monsieur de Montigny at Ragny. If you wish to make a good investment you should come and buy it for eight million in assignats. You could put up as deposit sixty thousand francs of your wife's dowry. I advise you to do this. Remember me to Julie and to Désirée and to all the family. I am sure you could buy the estate for eighty thousand francs in silver. Before the revolution it was worth two hundred and fifty thouand. It is a unique opportunity of investing some of Julie's dowry. Assignats decline in value daily.'

In his pocket Napoleon carried a lock of Désirée's hair and a letter she had put in his hand as they said goodbye: 'My only consolation is that I know you will always be faithful to me.' Of course he would be faithful, for on the table was his last letter: 'How could you imagine that I could cease loving you? Yours to the end of life.' Rash words, according to which his life was to end months later in the arms of Josephine de Beauharnais.

Joseph, who was in Marseille when he received the letter, did not take his brother's advice. Had he shown the letter to his shrewd mother or to his businesslike father-in-law either would have told him to spare at least a few days to visit Ragny. If the seller could have been persuaded to accept payment, or even part-payment, in those worthless pieces of paper issued by the Government so much the better. Issued at what today might correspond to four pounds assignats eventually became worth less than a penny. Kind, indolent Joseph Buonaparte, who, like his father, could look the part when dressed as a king, lacked all other essentials. The wisest things he did in life were to marry a rich wife and to escape to America when his brother's Empire crumbled and he could no longer be moved like a pawn from throne to throne.

Chapter 15

Pause in Paris

The three young officers and the youth accompanying them who booked rooms at the Hotel de la Liberté in Paris on the evening of 24 May 1795 looked out next morning upon a changing city. During the ten months since the death of Robespierre the political pendulum had swung back towards the middle; men had grown tired of rule by terror; the Jacobin party had become less popular; royalists no longer had to remain in hiding but walked head high.

The rue des Fossés, Montmartre, in which the hotel was situated, was not in the most fashionable part of Paris; its inhabitants were less aristocratic than their neighbours across the river in the Faubourg Saint Germain, but as the morning drew on well-dressed women could be seen passing the hotel accompanied by young men of breeding, wearing tightly-waisted tail-coats with exaggerated padded shoulders and excessively high collars known as anti-guillotine. Their knee-breeches were of silk, their stockings white, they wore wide winged hats over blond wigs. These were *les Muscadins*, so called after the scent they favoured, or alternatively *les Incoyables* from their habit of leaving out the 'r' whenever possible. Everything was *incoyable*, and no sentence seemed to be complete without an added *paole d'honneur*.

It was fashionable to carry a cudgel with which to threaten any of *le peuple* who dared to cross one's path. The mob was to be kept in its place.

The Committee of Public Safety was still in existence but in a modified form. Its claws had been cut. Exercising restricted power, it no longer inspired fear. The Revolution had not died with Robespierre, rather it had gone off the boil, allowing the scum to come to the top. Such men as Barras, Fréron, Fouché and Tallien now controlled the affairs of a France as poor as it had been five years ago when the States General had been called to the rescue. They were second-rate men, less dangerous but more corrupt than those they had brought down. They had little to offer but words. Robespierre, pursuing the path of truth, the rebirth of society, had been defeated by his own creed. Those who came after him aimed lower, their target was power accompanied by wealth. Integrity was a height from which one might fall with tragic result. Life was short. Why not make it as pleasant as possible? The poor would always be poor. Pacify them with promises and soft words, convince them that prosperity was on the way. Meanwhile grasp for oneself the comfort within reach. Hold fast to it with greedy hands. Greedy? No, they were the servants of the state, of the people, democratically elected by them. Those who questioned their authority questioned the rights of the people.

Yet only a few days before the arrival of the young officers at the Hotel de la Liberté the poor of Paris had risen in protest once again and had marched on the House of Representatives, as they had been encouraged to do over the past few years, and demanded justice. Famine had followed a winter so hard that carriages could drive across the Seine in safety. Driven by hunger and despair the mob broke into the Chamber crying 'Give us bread'. One member, Citizen Ferand, possibly nearest the door and endeavouring to resist the entrance of violent men, was killed. All were threatened. But the President, Boissy d'Anglas, managed to restore order by promising the invaders bread. Their anger appeased, they withdrew – without bread. Boissy d'Anglas had the gift of turning away wrath with a soft answer. He was known to those over whom he presided and to the hungry as Boissy-Famine.

This was the last occasion during the Revolution on which elected authority was challenged by the mob; on the next occasion the challenge would come from those who proclaimed themselves royalist. No ragged, *sans-culotte* mob this time, but well-fed, well-dressed men, angered by the guile of men seeking to retain office while they, the dispossessed, sought the restoration of their privileged status. This event comes later. But the young man who was destined to crush that rising, that final attempt to challenge the elected government had now arrived in Paris. He was unknown save to a few fellow soldiers who had seen him at work, or to one or two politicians such as Barras, Saliceti and Ricord – and the two latter were themselves now in trouble. Yet within a few weeks his name would be known to all France, within a year to all the world.

General Buonaparte's period of sick-leave was due to expire on 15 July but long before that date he went to live in the more modest surroundings of a third-rate hotel called Le Cadran Bleu in the narrow rue de la Huchette on the south bank of the Seine. His younger brother, Louis, as we know, soon afterwards entered the School of Artillery at Châlons and was therefore, for the time being at least, off his hands, but their mother, struggling to maintain the rest of the family in Marseille, was in dire need of help. Napoleon sent her every penny he could spare, retaining for himself only 3 francs a week, the cost of his room, and enough for one meal a day.

It was at this time that Buonaparte and his school friend de Bourrienne met again. Three years ago they had stood together in the Place du Carrousel where de Bourrienne's brother had a furniture shop, and had witnessed the sack of the Tuileries Palace and the massacre of the King's Swiss guards. They had seen the end of the French monarchy.

There was also a meeting, as important as that with de Bourrienne, with Des Mazis. They had been friends at the Paris Military School before the Revolution, and had joined the same regiment on the same day. The two had served together for some years; but when the Revolution increased in violence Des Mazis sent in his resignation and emigrated. Today, the worst being over, he had risked returning to Paris, prudently disguised as a labourer, to help his mother. Learning of his friend's distress, more especially of the distress of Madame Letitzia and her children in Marseille, he took some gold coins from a belt hidden beneath his workman's clothes and said 'Send it to your mother'. Napoleon took the money and ran. They were not to meet again for fifteen years, for Des Mazis preferred cultivating his garden to the pursuit of military glory. When by chance the Emperor came upon Des Mazis he asked, 'Why did you not come to see me and ask for the repayment of my debt?' to which Des Mazis replied, 'I did not need the money. I had enough.' It was with difficulty that Napoleon persuaded him to accept a repayment of ten times the original loan and the post of Director of the State Gardens which carried with it a salary of 30,000 francs a year.

There were at that time repeated visits to Madame Permon, a friend of Corsican days who had married a Frenchman and was now a widow living in Paris with her daughter, Laure. Perhaps it was a sense of loneliness, even of home-sickness for Corsica, that led him to propose marriage to Madame Permon. She refused him with kindness and tact. 'I am sure you have a great future before you but do remember that I am old enough to be your mother.' Captain Junot sometimes accompanied his chief on visits to the Permon's house and in his case all ended happily. Having failed with Pauline Buonaparte, he succeeded handsomely with Laure Permon, married her and afterwards made her the Duchess of Abrantès. In her memoirs, often criticized for inaccuracy but always entertaining, Laure left a picture of the Napoleon of those days, crossing the courtyard in threadbare uniform, boots down-at-heel, often uncleaned, his features drawn, his complexion sallow, his hair falling uncombed over his ears.

Meanwhile the authorities were rightly growing impatient. Sick leave was all very well, but there was a limit. If this officer wished to continue in the service it was time he learnt to accept discipline and obey orders. Perhaps sensing that the limit of official patience had been reached, Napoleon requested an interview with the War Minister himself, a certain Aubry, successor to the great Lazare Carnot whose creation of France's Revolutionary Armies had earned him the name of 'Organizer of Victory' and had saved him from execution in the days of the Terror. However, it was not enough to prevent his removal from office.

The interview was granted but was unpleasant and unproductive. Aubry, strongly anti-Jacobin, was in any case unlikely to offer a warm welcome to a youthful general who owed his rapid promotion to the favouritism of Augustin Robespierre and who had actually been imprisoned less than a year ago, accused of treacherous conduct. He was lucky to have been let out. By what right did he now consider himself entitled to a personal interview with the political head of the armed forces? He was already under orders to take up a command in the Army of the West. As and when opportunity offered he would be returned to his chosen arm of the service. Citizen Aubry also had on his desk a confidential report: 'This officer is a general of artillery of which branch of the service he has a thorough knowledge, but he is over-ambitious and too much given to intrigue to merit recommendation for promotion.'

The report was unlikely to help matters nor was the fact that Buonaparte had little respect for Aubry, who was also a gunner officer, but who had never risen above the rank of captain, preferring to hoist himself upward on the branches of the political tree. Arriving at the position of Minister of War he had promoted himself to Major-General and Inspector-General-of-Artillery. Rapid promotion indeed, carrying with it an equally rapid increase in income. To Aubry's rather foolish remark that Buonaparte was in any case too young a man to hold the rank of general the latter replied, 'One matures quickly on the field of battle'. Since Aubry had never been within sight or sound of battle the thrust was painful. It was time the interview came to an end. General Buonaparte received a direct order to rejoin his command without delay. He saluted his senior and bowed himself out, deter-mined not to obey.

Meanwhile Joseph, now in Genoa, received a continuous flow of letters from his brother in Paris:

> I will do what I can to find something for Lucien ... I am not well and am going to request an extension of sick-leave. When my health is better I will decide what to do ... Jerome has written asking me to find a school for him.

> I have not heard from you since you left [presumably for Genoa] nor has Désirée written to me. The English have landed 12,000 men, mostly French emigrants, in Brittany. The Army of the Pyrenees, also that of Italy, is under attack ... Bread is scarce in Paris. The gold louis rises in value every day. It is now worth 750 francs.

> The English will be forced to re-embark within a few days. Peace with Spain is imminent. Pichegru is preparing to cross the Rhine.

The English attack on Quiberon in Brittany was made early in July. It was badly planned and badly led. The bulk of the attacking force, as Buonaparte said, was composed of French emigrants. It failed miser-ably. Bad news had come shortly before from the Army of Italy – about the time of what might be called the Boissy-Famine rising in Paris. Kellermann, who had taken over command from Dumerbion, was driven back as far as Loano by the Austrians. However, the danger passed, owing to lack of initiative on the part of the Austrians.

Peace with Spain was signed during July and, in spite of the lack of bread and other necessities, in spite of the daily rise in the cost of living and hovering bankruptcy, a false prosperity swept over France, or at least over Paris. People spent whatever money they had, fearing it would buy less next day. The futility of saving filled men's hearts with despair. The aged awaited death with apathy, the young foresaw a hopeless future. And yet, as always, disaster was not universal. Many still appeared to be rich. Speculation of one sort or another had succeeded. Those whom it had favoured grew opulent, drove past in gilded carriages, arrogant, pitiless. Democracy had gone mad, anarchy hovered with spread wings.

Chapter 16

Hope in Paris

'If things go on like this I shall end by allowing myself to be run over by a passing carriage.' The words were written by Napoleon in the summer of 1795 to his elder brother, Joseph. He was then twenty-five years of age, and was confessing a feeling which at one period of life or another comes to many men and women.

Boissy d'Anglas had kept his word, but at a price: the hungry had been given bread, but only by requisitioning the crops of hard-working peasants in exchange for worthless bits of paper. Everything contributed to the despair of thinking men. The populace were desperate because revolution so rich in promise had proved so poor in result. Wealth had merely changed hands, power its residence. The high hopes which, five years ago, had coloured the future had faded.

Nearer at hand family news contributed to Napoleon's state of depression. Madame Mère and the three girls were ekeing out a meagre existence in a poor quarter of Marseille, little Jerome was without education and Uncle Fesch was still out of work. Worst of all Lucien had been tracked down to his hiding place in Sète and arrested and imprisoned at Aix-en-Provence with others of Jacobin sympathy. His wife and their five-month-old child were meanwhile left dependent upon her uncle or the charity of neighbours at Saint Maximin. Lucien was released from prison after a few weeks thanks to the untiring efforts of his mother, added to those of his brother in Paris, but he was now penniless. All in all it was a bad time for the Buonaparte family, the only exception being Joseph who had married money and now spent most of his days in neutral Genoa comfortably removed from political strife.

It was now in the darkest moment that, as so often happens, a light shone out of nowhere. It shone, where it could only shine with effect, upon the path of General Buonaparte. The first outward sign of a change of fortune came on 1 August when Citizen Aubry was removed from office. The new Minister of War was of aristocratic descent, his name – Louis-Gustave Le Doulcet, Comte de Pontécoulant, and one may ask how, with such a name, he had survived the days of the Terror. Perhaps because, when chosen to act as counsel for the defence of Charlotte Corday, he had declined the brief. That would have brought him into favour with Marat's friends, in other words ninety percent of *le peuple*. If accused of moral courage he could in any case plead, 'My decision was only premature. Soon afterwards the Law of Prairial forbade any counsel for the defence of those brought for trial before the Revolutionary Tribunal.'

Two days before the change of Minister of War Buonaparte received an alarming communication. His leave of absence upon grounds of health had gone on long enough. Either he must take up his command in the Army of the West as directed earlier in the year or be considered as unfit for military duty. The authorities had had enough.

His reply was another impertinent request for an interview at the War Ministry which, surprisingly, was granted. He appeared before Doulcet de Pontécoulant who listened patiently and attentively, not only when he pleaded his case, but with increasing interest, when, feeling the atmosphere favourable, he outlined his plan for a spirited attack by a reinforced Army of Italy upon the Austrians and the Piedmontese in northern Italy, followed by the total expulsion of the Austrian Army from that country. The Minister of War suggested that such an ambitious plan of campaign merited further thought. Would General Buonaparte put his ideas in writing and de Pontécoulant would personally bring them to the notice of the Committee of Public Safety. Buonaparte sat himself at the table and hastily outlined the plan he was destined to put into operation eight months later when he led his army almost to the gates of Vienna.

General Kellermann, having relinquished command of the Army of the Alps, now commanded that of Italy. Buonaparte was instructed to transmit his ideas to him. The instructions to General Kellermann were signed by the President of the Committee of Public Safety which allowed freedom of expression and forcible suggestions for the future activity of his army. They were, however, without result. The Army of Italy, for the most part underpaid, ragged, lacking transport and provisions, even boots for the men, was forced to remain on the defensive. Its leader was, in any case, soon to be replaced by another general, Schérer.

One other event in that summer of 1795 was to make its contribution to the future career of Napoleon. In June a little boy died in the Temple prison. His only crime was that he was the son of a king; he was *le Dauphin*, heir to the throne of France. He was ten years old. Born in the luxury of Versailles he and his parents had left the palace for the last time on a September afternoon when he was four. They had driven to Paris surrounded by a raucous mob crying, 'We are bringing the baker home. Now we shall have bread.' Residence in the Tuileries Palace in Paris had been followed by imprisonment in the Temple, from where he had seen, first his father, and a few months later his mother, led away to death. The love of parents had been replaced by the companionship of a brutal, illiterate shoemaker, his name Simon, whose duty it was to make of the child a 'Patriotic Citizen'. Death had rescued the little boy from unkindly fate. Known in royalist France, in particular in Toulon, as Louis XVII, he might have barred the way of Napoleon to the Empire. He could well have become a magnet for Frenchmen who desired a return to constitutional monarchy.

The heir to the throne was now the brother of Louis XVI, later to be known as Louis XVIII. At the time a fugitive, surrounded by a make-believe court, he issued from Verona a proclamation threatening dire punishment to any who had taken part in the Revolution and promising the restitution of their property to its victims. Poor Louis had learnt nothing from adversity. He now lost an opportunity of retrieving much. For the opportunity was there. French opinion was changing. People were tired of violence. To what had it led? Reasoned argument and toleration were, after all, preferable. A government headed by a hereditary monarch promised hope. It could not be worse. There had come about in France what today would be called a swing to the right. But faced with the stubborn, unseeing mind of Louis XVIII, what hope was there for any statesman of moderate views? None.

Chapter 17

Back to work

General Buonaparte was back in circulation. Appointed by de Pontécoulant to the *Bureau Typographique* – which may be compared to the planning department of a modern general staff – he was frequently in contact with higher authority, discussing with members of the Government the future activities of the various armies protecting the frontiers of France. He also received flattering invitations to social gatherings and found himself at receptions and dinner parties in the houses of the supposedly great, for though the country might be heading for bankruptcy the rich were still present.

Buonaparte lost no time in getting down to work, in drafting plans for the employment of the armed forces, in particular for that of the Army of Italy spread out along the Riviera coast. But this was not enough. It was no more than a stepping stone for ambition. He could suggest, advise, criticize, but he could not order. Active and impatient, his mind overflowed with ideas. His eyes looked towards the magic East which ever drew him. Why, one may ask, when there was more than enough to occupy his fertile brain in France?

The East! Why not send a military mission to Turkey with himself in command? The Sultan was reputed to be seeking advice, more particularly in regard to his artillery. Napoleon put forward the idea and the Committee accepted it – perhaps because it was thought that Turkey might prove a valuable ally in any dispute with the British who not only had eyes on the East but possessions in it.

Overjoyed at the prospect of being set free from the restraints of higher authority, of being able to use his initiative in what was then a far-off country he allowed his enthusiasm to overflow towards Joseph. 'I will have them appoint you Consul.'

There was, however, to be no diplomatic appointment for Joseph, for no Military Mission ever set off for Turkey. Almost on the day when authority was given for its creation (Junot, Marmont and others of the faithful were of course to be included) Buonaparte received notice of his dismissal from the army, the reason given being his refusal to take up his command with the Army of the West. In reality that matter was finished, but administrative correspondence moves slowly. The communication had pursued its unhurried way through various War Office departments until it reached its destination.

Coincidentally de Pontécoulant also received a notice of dismissal. He had only been in office a few weeks, but the Committee of Public Safety, though no longer dangerous, still enjoyed pulling strings to make its servants jump. Aubry, who also had a short reign, had been too anti-Jacobin; de Pontécoulant was too enlightened, too popular. It is, however, pleasant to know that before departing he handed his successor a report full of praise for General Buonaparte: 'I recommend him to my colleagues as a citizen of the Republic who can be employed with profit in the Artillery or in any other branch of the Service.'

Meanwhile, what of Désirée Clary waiting sadly hopefully in faraway Marseille? She must often have left her comfortable home to visit the Buonapartes living a threadbare existence in the slums of the Vieux Port at the end of La Cannebière. Had Madame Mère received news of Napoleon recently? Désirée knew well enough that her family did not wish her to marry him but now that he had been given important work in the War Office with the promise of promotion, surely they would relent. Désirée herself could do nothing but remain faithful to her faithless lover. Until he made a formal request for her hand she was powerless. And he made no request. The allurements of Parisian society were cooling his already tepid ardour. Invitations to the salons of popular hostesses had begun to reach him. He was welcomed in the homes of such women as Madame Récamier, the banker's wife, and of course in that of Notre-Dame de Thermidor. The insincere flattery of the salons and the mature charm of Madame Permon contributed to forgetfulness of Marseille. It might have been expected; for when in Nice the nearness of Marseille had not deterred him from asking for the hand of fifteen-year-old Emilia Laurenti while at the same time protesting undying love for Désirée. Yet he should not be judged too harshly. Mature in intellect far beyond his years Napoleon at twenty-five was emotionally immature; he was not in love with the person, he was in love with love.

> The day before yesterday I dined at Madame Tallien's. She is getting rather old, but she would have loved you had she known you. A score of women were there and I have never seen such an unattractive crowd.

Was it a sense of guilt which made Napoleon write this to Désirée? It could not, however alter the fading of love.

'How can I ever be happy without you?' coming from Désirée sounded a truer, deeper note. When she read in reply, 'I have received your charming letter, my dear friend,' her heart must have felt a sudden chill. It was a far cry from the days of 'Yours to the end of life'.

Storm clouds were now gathering over Paris and spreading outwards. The political situation had again become threatening. Twelve months had passed since the death of Robespierre and from the Convention had come only half-promises and talk. Tyranny had of necessity been destroyed, but in its place had come only a void. The men who had destroyed tyranny, the Thermidoreans, had proved sadly disappointing: those who had brains were self-seeking, those who had none tamely waited for the crumbs of office to fall.

The National Convention, truly enough elected by universal suffrage, after four years had grown stale. Its heart no longer beat. It was time for a change. A committee formed to consider what was to be done produced an idea for a change which was no change, merely a political manoeuvre. The Convention would be dissolved, or would dissolve itself, the nation would be consulted and should vote, but whatever the wishes of the electorate two thirds of the present members of the Convention should retain their seats in what would then be called the Directory – brilliant. So brilliant as to be transparent. When the idea was put to an impatient public only a small part voted and of that small part only one in five voted in favour.

In September discontent rose to boiling point; in the first week of October it boiled over. Rumour and counter-rumour warned of voilence. The convention which had encouraged mob-rule now saw that rule employed against itself; and this time insurrection was not confined to hungry, ill-clad, fist-raising men. There was no longer a Tuileries to be entered and sacked. A certain Citizen Damican had mustered some 20,000 armed men – and part of the National Guard joined him – ready to march on the Convention. Many were royalists, deprived, envious men ready to join in any form of violence in the hope of gain, or merely for the fun of it.

Barras, who had been five years a soldier, was chosen by the frightened members of the Convention to protect them, and to maintain Government, such as it was, in being. The alternative was too terrible to contemplate. Were they to end as Royalty had ended? As the victims of the Terror had ended?

This was on 5 October 1795, known at the time as 13 Vendemiaire of the year IV, a day to be remembered not only because it put an end to the French Revolution but because it sounded the entry upon the political scene of the man destined to tower head and shoulders above all who followed him or crowded round him on the stage of Europe.

Chapter 18

Success in Paris

General Menou, commanding the Army of the Interior at this time, was a soldier of experience, but by nature timid and slow to act. With the 5,000 men of the Paris garrison he was not the man to challenge 30,000 men, of whom two thirds belonged to the National Guard, and were therefore trained up to a point and fully armed. On 5 October whole battalions were making ready to march on the centre of government. This was no mere mob rising; it was Civil War.

Menou's first move was to open negotiations with a battalion of the National Guard which had taken over the Convent of The Daughters of Saint Thomas where the Paris Stock Exchange now stands. He tried to calm the occupants of the convent by suggesting they should hand over their arms and go home. When they did neither, it became clear to the members of the Convention that if they wished to remain in power, or even alive, more decisive leadership was necessary. They turned to Barras. His experience as a subaltern in the Regiment of Pondicherry was of no particular value now, but he had at least risked his life in bringing down Robespierre and thereby saved theirs. Barras was made Commander in Chief of the Army of the Interior.

But the restoration of order was not going to be easy, he would need a capable assistant. There are many versions of how Buonaparte came to be chosen as second-in-command to Barras. That related by Barras himself may be disregarded; he was never at any time truthful, nor did he have any love for Buonaparte after the latter became First Consul and he was pushed into the shadows.

No doubt the words of Napoleon spoken twenty years later on Saint Helena relate the events of the day as accurately as any. On 5 October he was, he said, lunching with Madame Permon. Excitement in the city ran high; they discussed the political situation – which no doubt meant listening to his version of it – and he left her, with the intention of finding out at first hand what was happening and returning later to inform her. He did not return, and it is recorded that he went that night to the Théâtre Fydeau from where he was fetched by a messenger whose instructions were to conduct him to Barras, then directing operations from the Tuileries.

This seems most unlikely. Setting off from the Permon house after luncheon, entering upon a scene of turmoil – Paris streets echoing to the beating of drums, to cries of 'Down with the Two Thirds', to men calling on all and sundry to join the revolt, while from Montmartre came the sound of shooting – it is difficult to visualize Buonaparte calmly going to the theatre. It is easier to believe that at the end of the day he went, as he said, to the House of Representatives to ascertain what steps were to be taken to cope with the disorder. Many members were for withdrawing the troops and seeking peace without the risk of bloodshed. Perhaps it was to counter this that one member, recognizing Buonaparte, proposed him as assistant to Barras. Perhaps it was Fréron (still hoping for Pauline's hand) or Turreau; both were present.

He was taken to Barras who offered him the job, giving him a few seconds in which to accept or refuse. He accepted, adding, 'If I take it on I shall stop at nothing until order is restored.' There were to be no half measures. Armed now with authority his first thought was 'guns', without which his 5,000 men could hardly stand against four or five times their number.

A young cavalry officer, Murat, was at hand. He was ordered to take 200 troopers, ride top-speed to the Sablon Plain (now part of residential Neuilly) and seize the forty guns parked there. It was known that the insurgents, too, were after them; it was a race against time. But none better than Murat could have been chosen, later to become Napoleon's brother-in-law and King of Naples. Later still to be shot by a firing squad: 'Not on the face, please. Aim for the heart.' He brought back the guns on time.

There was fighting that day not only near the Church of Saint Roch in the rue Saint Honoré, but on the bridges crossing the Seine, in various quarters of the city. Napoleon was here, there and everywhere. In the late afternoon he stood behind the two guns facing the church. He had not opened fire, preferring to await an attack which must come if the rebels were to achieve success. Here was the critical point, a stone's throw from the Tuileries where some eight hundred Representatives of the People waited, each armed with a pistol provided by him. Would it really come to this? To hand-to-hand fighting with the people whose interests they had been elected to represent? Many of them had never even held a pistol before, let alone fired one. But they need not have feared. The master soldier was at hand.

A shot was fired from the church. The two guns opened fire at point blank range, killing some two hundred, wounding many more. The rest fled. This was the 'whiff of grapeshot' which blew the last remnants of the French Revolution to smithereens. The members of the Convention breathed again; nor could they do enough for the man who had saved them. The government of France still governed. Their gratitude overflowed.

That night the hero recorded in simple words the events of the day:

> The Committee appointed me Second-in Command. We positioned our men. The enemy attacked us near the Tuileries. We killed many of them.

Three days later General Buonaparte was promoted to the rank of Major-General; two weeks later, Paul Barras, having been elected a member of the newly created Directory which was to govern France very badly for the next four years, handed over to him the command of the Army of the Interior.

The new Commander-in-Chief was now installed in the rue des Capucines, from where some of his windows gave on to the Place Vendôme. Today his statue dominates that square from the top of a tall column. He had risen from poverty to affluence in a day. A well equipped home (an official residence paid for by the State), servants, horses, grooms, secretaries were all suddenly his. Immediately he thought of the family. He petitioned for a post as Consul in Italy for Joseph, had Lucien made a Commissioner of Army Supplies – a lucrative position. Louis was promoted to the rank of first lieutenant and brought to Paris as his brother's Aide-de-Camp. Jerome was sent to a good school. Money suddenly flowed toward Madame Mère and the girls.

One of Buonaparte's first orders was that all arms must be handed in, that any person found in possession of arms would in future incur the death penalty.

> While Commander of Paris [it is from de Bourrienne that we have this] a boy of ten or twelve, Eugène, the son of viscount Beauharnais who had been put to death by Robespierre, visited the General and asked for the retention of his father's sword. Buonaparte complied with his request. The boy's tears of gratitude as he received permission touched Buonaparte's heart and he treated him kindly. Next day the boy's mother, Josephine de Beauharnais, came to thank the General. Her beauty and her exceptional gracefulness made a strong impression on him. The acquaintance thus begun speedily led to their marriage.

There are other versions of how Buonaparte came to know Josephine. This one will do for the moment. It has a romantic sound; it may well be true. What matters is the fact that it was now, when he had at last achieved a position of importance and of promise, that Josephine came into Napoleon's life.

From the rue des Capucines came a continuous stream of orders. It was apparent to every officer and man of the Army of the Interior, in particular to the Paris garrison, that an energetic, knowledgeable mind was at work, enquiring, criticizing, directing, that no small detail was overlooked or ignored. True leadership was at the helm.

The Bureau Typographique was not far away and was certainly not to be forgotten. General Schérer, now in command of the Army of Italy, was pestered with enquiries and recommendations. Winter was approaching. Why could not the authorities in Paris, far from the scene, leave things to him. He was not aware at the time of the authorship of this disturbing correspondence, for Buonaparte, going outside his immediate duties, submitted all to the five members of the Directory, using them as his mouthpiece. Recognizing the value of his remarks, they forwarded them without hesitation. On 11 December a letter recommended in strong terms the capture of Ceva as being essential in persuading the Piedmontese to make peace. This was followed in January 1796 by:

If the Army of Italy, wastes the month of February, as it has January, the Italian campaign will be ruined ... the Army must advance on Ceva, and capture it before the Austrians can get there and link up with the Piedmontese.

General Schérer became increasingly hostile to whoever was handing out this sort of advice. His reply was a demand for reinforcements. At last things came to a head. Schérer suggested that the hair-brained idiot who was constantly recommending action impossible of execution from an arm-chair in Paris should himself try to carry it out. He then resigned his command. On 2 March his resignation was accepted. On the same day General Buonaparte was offered command of the Army of Italy. His way lay open. His dream had come true. As if to emphasize his good fortune he changed the spelling of his name from Buonaparte to Bonaparte.

Chapter 19

Josephine and Fame

Marie Joseph Rose de Tascher de la Pagerie, destined to become empress of the First French Empire, was born in the West Indies, on the island of Martinique, brought to France by an aunt when she was sixteen and married to the Vicomte Alexandre de Beauharnais, whose father had been goveror of the island. Rose – she was not known as Josephine until later – and Alexandre had been friends in childhood; they were, however, far from being friends when married. When the Revolution broke out ten years later Alexandre was a general in the French army, Rose the mother of two children, Eugène and Hortense.

Living separate lives, Rose and her husband found themselves in 1793, the year of terror, brought together in the Carmes Prison, a monastery until the year before when the monks had been massacred. Though friendly in adversity, each sought consolation in the arms of another: Alexandre in those of beautiful Delphine de Custine, Rose in those of General Hoche. Soon enough death came for Alexandre, who, tearing himself from the embrace of Delphine, still found time to write farewell words of gratitude and affection to his wife.

It must have seemed to Rose de Beauharnais that General Hoche, too, was on his way to the guillotine when soon afterwards he was transferred to the *Conciergerie*, usually the last stop on the way to execution. But Hoche survived and afterwards served his country with distinction. Today his statue looks down upon the courtyard of the Invalides.

Rose de Beauharnais – we may as well call her Josephine from now on – remained a prisoner in the Carmes, incessantly dealing the cards to learn her fate, shedding hysterical tears (courage was not among her qualities), cold with fear each evening lest her name be read out among those who were to die tomorrow. Once a name was called there was no hope: the Law of Prairial had been voted. Fouquier-Tinville, absolved from the tiresome necessity of listening to counsel for the defence, was now sending a stream of victims to the scaffold at ever increasing speed.

But luck was on the side of Josephine. Less than a week after the fall of Robespierre she was freed from prison. Years ago, in Martinique, a fortune-teller had studied the palm of her hand: 'You will be greater than a queen', she had been told. On the day in July 1794 that Josephine stepped out of the Carmes prison she started on her way to the throne. When she was told she was free it is said she fainted gracefully. Josephine did everything gracefully; smiles, tears, honeyed words, a graceful carriage and kindness were her weapons, and she used them to effect.

Free now, all the more free for having known the imminent threat of death, she rapidly regained her desire for the good things of life: fine clothes, good food, elegant surroundings, superficial friends with whom to exchange superficial conversation. Also one must have servants and a carriage. A *vicomtesse* could not be expected to live like *le peuple*. Then there were the children to feed and clothe and educate. Robespierre was dead, terror had died with him, the world of fashion was going to be happy ever after, provided of course one had money. And money could only come from rich and generous men, men in power who could reach out for it. If their generosity had a price, well, one could always appear suitably shocked or bargain gracefully.

Her most recent conquest being General Hoche, it was to him that Josephine first turned, only to find disappointment. Hoche, to quieten her demands, promised to make room on his staff for her son Eugène, but as the boy was still only thirteen this did not amount to much. Not a step further would Hoche go. An affair in prison when nobody knew what the morrow might bring could be pardoned or at least understood. Expensive adultery in a free world, more especially when he had a loved and loving wife could find no excuse. Hoche was no easy game. He was even heard to refer to Josephine as a *catin* – a strumpet – an ungrateful remark, let fall no doubt in a moment forgetful of pleasure shared.

Undeterred, Josephine pursued her way towards the good things of life. She must be out and about. Solitude was abhorrent to her. She must have social success, the smiles of women friends, the adulation of men, especially of rich men, among whom was Paul Barras, at that time the richest of all.

Madame Tallien, whom Josephine had known before the Terror, gave her the entry into Parisian society, such as it was. In the home of Notre-Dame de Thermidor she met Paul Barras, President of the National Convention in succession to Boissy d'Anglas (a far more honest man), immensely rich, corrupt and powerful. Scandalous talk soon had it that Josephine de Beauharnais was the mistress of Paul Barras. Nobody can know the truth, but it is certain that Barras was not the man to show disinterested generosity, and that about this time Josephine installed herself in a charming house, 3 rue Chantereine, furnished with luxury and taste. Also, though the widow of an Army Officer and of small means, she was allowed credit on a large scale. She was in fact as full of debts as of charm. The fact that Barras, the man of the day, was her friend, was sufficient collateral.

More than a year went by between Josephine's release from prison and the historic day of Vendemiaire when General Buonaparte was called upon to assist Paul Barras in quelling the armed rising which threatened not only the government but the lives of its members. It is possible, as Eugène de Beauharnais recounts in his memoirs, that it was soon after he was given permission to retain his father's sword that his mother, calling to express her gratitude, made the acquaintance of Napoleon. It is more probable that she had already met him at Madame Tallien's home, though at the time she would not have been impressed. But after Vendemiaire, when General Buonaparte's name was on everybody's lips, it was another matter. Her liaison with Barras was nearing an end. Wisdom therefore dictated that she kept her eyes open for a successor.

Josephine did not have to look further than Madame Tallien's drawing-room, where all Paris gathered, including General Buonaparte. She was interested, he captivated. At a dinner party, Hortense de Beauharnais records, she found herself sitting between her mother and the General. He talked incessantly across her so that she had constantly to sit back, which she found annoying. During the early days, in any case, neither Hortense nor her brother welcomed the idea of their mother re-marrying, but that was to pass as they grew up and their step-father became increasingly famous.

Meanwhile love pursued its course. In December Josephine, who perhaps had not been giving enough encouragement of late to Buonaparte, or perhaps feeling he might slip away, sent him a note:

> Why do you never come to visit your friend who is so fond of you? You have quite deserted her. Why not come tomorrow for lunch? I should love to see you and have a good talk with you about your future.
>
> Je vous embrasse,
Veuve Beauharnais

Of course he went. The name Barras came into the conversation: 'He and I are only good friends, you know that don't you?' If Buonaparte thought differently he was quite ready to believe her. It made subsequent reference to Barras less embarrassing. And it was very necessary to talk of Barras, who had it in his power to appoint generals to the command of armies.

That luncheon in the rue Chantereine in December 1795 has its place in history. From that day onward Napoleon was ensnared. No more Désirée, no more anybody. Only Josephine who (he confided to a friend), had the most beautiful *petit derrière* you ever saw.

Whether Josephine did suggest to Barras that Napoleon should succeed Schérer in command of the Army of Italy is not known. It is certain, however, that Napoleon consulted Barras about his marriage – told Barras of his decision would be more accurate. Barras fully approved. And when on 2 March 1796 Napoleon was given command of that army, it was whispered by the jealous or the mischievous that it was a wedding present from Barras, delighted to have Josephine taken off his hands.

On 8 March Napoleon married Josephine. Tallien and Barras were of course present and heard him add eighteen months to his age and deduct four years from that of his bride.

'How could you treat a poor maiden so,' was the theme of Désirée's letter, written when she heard the news. 'I shall never marry, never.' But she did, two and a half years later. Later still she and her husband were made Prince and Princess of Ponté-Corvo by the Emperor Napoleon who could never resist elevating friends and relatives to thrones, real or imaginary – a less harmful exercise of Imperial power than sending men to death on the battlefields of Europe.

Three days after their marriage the lover bowed his way out and the man of action entered upon the scene. General Bonaparte his ADC, Captain Junot, seated beside him in the carriage, set off from the rue Chantereine to assume command of the Army of Italy. Josephine shed suitable tears, waved good-bye to her 'funny little husband' and turned to the pleasures of Paris. To accompany him would have been asking too much. Long hours of jolting on half-paved roads, nights in wayside inns, perhaps even in a tent, were not for her. Again, how could she possibly tear herself away from all those dear friends – more especially from dashing young Hippolyte Charles, so attractive in his cavalry officer's uniform, so ardent when he shed it? There were the children to be thought of too. She did, however, promise to join her husband as soon as the military and political situation in Italy made this possible.

Napoleon did not take the shortest route to the headquarters of his army, but turned off at Aix-en-Provence to visit his mother in Marseille. To her surprise – for he had travelled faster than the post – she then learnt of his marriage. Gossip had no doubt already reached Marseille of his admiration for a woman of fashion in Paris, but that he should so suddenly announce his marriage came as a bitter shock. Well-brought-up Corsican children did not behave with so little respect for their parents. And who was the woman? A widow of questionable conduct, six years older than he, and with two children for whose future he would henceforth be responsible. He must have lost his head. It had been bad enough when Lucien married without her consent, but why should Nabulio have made such a fuss about that and then do the same himself?

Napoleon had brought with him a letter addressed to his mother from her new daughter-in-law. Madame Mère, after a suitable delay, answered the letter with cold dignity: 'My son has duly informed me of his marriage. It follows that, as his wife, you have my regard – etcetera, etcetera. It now only remains for me to look forward to the pleasure of making your acquaintance.'

After saying good-bye to his mother, whose feelings, despite the disappointing news of his marriage, must nevertheless have been softened by gratitude for all that he had done for the family since his promotion to the rank of Major-General in the previous October, Napoleon made for Toulon, the scene of his first success. Then on to Nice via Antibes, where he possibly glanced towards the fort with an indulgent smile, but where, more important than any memories of captivity, or of life with the family at Château Sallé, was his meeting with General Berthier, then Chief-of-Staff of the Army of Italy, and destined to serve him with incomparable efficiency during the coming years. Destined also to become a Marshal-of-France and Prince of Neuchâtel, and, alas, to die a tragic death in Bavaria – perhaps by his own hand – two weeks after the battle of Waterloo. Had he been present as Chief-of-Staff instead of Soult during that brief campaign, his long experience, his genius for detailed accuracy, might have delayed defeat; it could not have avoided disaster.

At Nice the four divisional commanders of the Army of Italy – Masséna, Sérurier, Augereau and Laharpe – waited to greet their new chief. Masséna knew him, or of him, from Toulon two years ago. To the others he came as a stranger, younger than any of them, inexperienced in the command of large forces. The four generals became increasingly suspicious of their new commander when, with childish and amorous enthusiasm, he produced a portrait of his wife for them to admire. Such conduct seemed to betray an immature mind. But the mind was only immature in matters of the heart. When in rapid succession questions followed as to the exact strength, equipment, firing-power, of each unit of each division, as to the situation regarding rations and pay, the enthusiastic lover sank into the ground, the professional soldier rose in his place. The four generals stiffened in their saddles. Here was no novice, no youthful protégé of a political party, here was a soldier who knew what soldiering was about.

The four generals had not removed their plumed hats when greeting Bonaparte. He removed his, they then did likewise. He replaced his hat, they remained uncovered. It was a moment of truth. 'Tomorrow I shall inspect each division', he said. 'On the day following we shall march.'

Whether or not this new Commander-in-Chief could succeed where other, far more experienced, generals, such as Dumerbion, Kellermann or Schérer, had decided that with such an ill-equipped, heartless, undisciplined army, static defence was alone possible, might well be questioned. What was no longer questionable to the four divisional commanders was that from now on attack was the word. Victory might or might not follow attack. Dynamic action was certain. They returned to their respective commands hopeful of tomorrow. They now had a leader.

The master had arrived at his point of departure from which there was to be no turning back; but he still found time to write daily letters of passionate love, sometimes twice a day, to his beloved. Answers to Napoleon's letters were rare and unresponsive. 'During the past four weeks I have received only two letters from you, each of three lines,' he wrote.

On 2 April 1796 he told his divisional commanders that the offensive against the Austrians and the Piedmontese would be launched on the 15th. To induce a sense of discipline in his army he disbanded one regiment and obtained, by borrowing, an issue of pay for his troops. An oath to serve one's country was all very well, but one must live. Here was a general who understood. Officers and men marched towards Italy with lightened steps.

> Soldiers you are ill-clad, hungry, the Government owes you much but can offer you nothing ... you lack boots and clothing, even rations ... the enemy has everything. It is for us to advance and seize it.

Whether these were Napoleon's exact words matters not. A new spirit lived in every soldier's heart. One of the most successful military campaigns the world has known had begun. A master of war was about to lead an army in a campaign brilliant in conception, unmatched in execution, decisive in result. That success in war is an illusion, never finally decisive, like other great warriors, Napoleon had still to learn.

Although he had warned that the offensive against the Austrian and Piedmontese would begin on 15 April already on the 12th Napoleon had fought and won his first battle at Montenotte.

A detailed description of the manoeuvres and battles which followed that first victory does not form part of this story. It is sufficient to record that within two weeks by speed, determination, the ability to follow the summing-up of a situation by instant action, and by taking risks which many would consider unjustifiable, General Bonaparte, not yet twenty-seven years of age, had forced the Piedmontese Army to lay down its arms and ask for an armistice. He might well issue a jubilant bulletin:

> Soldiers. In fifteen days you have gained six victories, taken 21 colours, 55 guns, seized several fortresses and conquered the richest parts of Piedmont.

The French losses were reported to be 6,000, those of the Piedmontese 25,000. The 1,000 men of General Augereau's division who had begun the campaign without muskets must have been highly pleased when, after the first battle, they were handed more than enough captured from the enemy.

It was now the turn of the Austrians, and this of course was a more serious, more lengthy matter, ending only twelve months later when the advanced guard of Napoleon's Army halted almost within sight of Vienna. During those months the names of victorious battles had echoed back to France like a joyous pealing of bells: Lodi, triumphant entry into Milan, Rivoli, Arcola, Castiglione, Verona, Mantua.

Fame crowned Napoleon Bonaparte, power destroyed him, love eluded him. Twenty-five years later, when he lay dying on the island of Saint Helena, those who stood at the bedside heard the voice which many admired and others feared, which had ordered the fate of millions, had made and unmade kings, whisper faintly to coming death: 'Josephine.'

Bibliography

Hon D. A. Bingham, *Selection from Letters and Despatches of Napoleon I*, (3 vols) Chapman and Hall, 1884

F. de Bourrienne, *Memoirs*, Hutchinson

Jean Burnat, E. Wanty, G. H. Dumont, *Le Dossier Napoléon*, Éditions Gerard et Cie Verviers, 1962

Gérard Caillet, *Le Journal de Napoléon*, Editions Denoël, 1978

André Castelot, (trans. G. Daniels) *Napoleon*, Harper & Row, 1973

David Chandler, *The Campaigns of Napoleon*, Weidenfeld & Nicolson, 1967

Joseph Chiari, *Corsica: Columbus's Isle*, Barrie and Rockliff, 1960,

Dormer Chreston, *In Search of Two Characters*, Macmillan, 1945

Alfred Cobhan, *History of Modern France*, (3 Vols) Penguin 1957

L. De Brotonne, *Dernières Lettres Inédites de Napoléon I*, Honoré Champion, Paris, 1903

L. De Brotonne, *Lettres Inédites de Napoléon I*, Honoré Champion, Paris, 1898

Pierson Dixon, *Pauline: Napoleon's Favourite Sister*, Collins, 1964

Sir John Elliot, *The Way of the Tumbrils*, Reinhardt, 1963

C. S. Forester, *Nelson*, The Bodley Head, 1929

Jean Paul Garnier, *L'Extrordinaire Destin des Bonaparte*, Librairie Academique Perrin, 1968

Walter Geer, *Napoleon and his Family*, Allen and Unwin, 1923

John Eldred Howard, (ed) *Letters and Documents of Napoleon*, Barrie

and Jenkins, 1961
Emil Ludwig, *Napoleon*, Boni and Liveright, New York, 1926
Louis Madelin, *La Jeunesse de Bonaparte*, Hachette, 1937
Tancred Martel, *Mémoires et Oeuvres de Napoléon*, Albin Michel, Paris, 1910
Napoléon: Collection. Génies et Réalités, Hachette, 1961
Suzanne Normand, *Telle fut Josephine*, Editions du Sud, 1962
E. Picard and L. Tuety, *Correspondance Inédit Conservé aux Archives de la Guerre*, H. Charles-Lavauzelle, Paris, 1912–25
J. Holland Rose, *Life of Napoleon*, G. Bell and Sons, 1924
Lord Rosebery, *Napoleon: The Last Phase*, Arthur L. Humphreys, 1906
Bernard Rouget, *Bonaparte à Nice*, Editions de Gourcez, 1977
Robert Southey, *Life of Nelson*, Dent
Monica Sterling, *A Pride of Lions*, Collins, 1961
Reay Tannahil, (ed) *Paris in the Revolution; Eye Witness Accounts*, The Folio Society
Ian Bentley Thompson, *Corsica*, David and Charles, 1971
J. M. Thompson, (trans) *Selected Letters of Napoleon*, Dent
Peter Thrasher, *Pasquali Paoli: An Enlightened Hero*, Constable, 1970
Geoffrey Wagner, *Elegy for Corsica*, Cassell, 1968
Marion Ward, *The Dubarry Inheritance*, Chatto and Windus, 1967
Peter Young, *Napoleon's Marshals*, Osprey, 1973

Index